I0046448

A Guide to Billing and Collecting Public Enterprise Utility Fees for Water, Wastewater, and Solid Waste Services

Kara A. Millonzi

UNC
SCHOOL OF GOVERNMENT

THE UNIVERSITY
of NORTH CAROLINA
at CHAPEL HILL

The School of Government at the University of North Carolina at Chapel Hill works to improve the lives of North Carolinians by engaging in practical scholarship that helps public officials and citizens understand and improve state and local government. Established in 1931 as the Institute of Government, the School provides educational, advisory, and research services for state and local governments. The School of Government is also home to a nationally ranked graduate program in public administration and specialized centers focused on information technology, environmental finance, and civic education for youth.

As the largest university-based local government training, advisory, and research organization in the United States, the School of Government offers up to 200 courses, seminars, and specialized conferences for more than 12,000 public officials each year. In addition, faculty members annually publish approximately fifty books, book chapters, bulletins, and other reference works related to state and local government. Each day that the General Assembly is in session, the School produces the *Daily Bulletin*, which reports on the day's activities for members of the legislature and others who need to follow the course of legislation.

The Master of Public Administration Program is a full-time, two-year program that serves up to sixty students annually. It consistently ranks among the best public administration graduate programs in the country, particularly in city management. With courses ranging from public policy analysis to ethics and management, the program educates leaders for local, state, and federal governments and nonprofit organizations.

Operating support for the School of Government's programs and activities comes from many sources, including state appropriations, local government membership dues, private contributions, publication sales, course fees, and service contracts. Visit www.sog.unc.edu or call 919.966.5381 for more information on the School's courses, publications, programs, and services.

Michael R. Smith, DEAN
Thomas H. Thornburg, SENIOR ASSOCIATE DEAN
Frayda S. Bluestein, ASSOCIATE DEAN FOR PROGRAMS
Todd A. Nicolet, ASSOCIATE DEAN FOR INFORMATION TECHNOLOGY
Ann Cary Simpson, ASSOCIATE DEAN FOR DEVELOPMENT AND COMMUNICATIONS
Bradley G. Volk, ASSOCIATE DEAN FOR ADMINISTRATION

FACULTY

Gregory S. Allison	Joseph E. Hunt	William C. Rivenbark
David N. Ammons	Willow S. Jacobson	Dale J. Roenigk
Ann M. Anderson	Robert P. Joyce	John Rubin
A. Fleming Bell, II	Kenneth L. Joyner	John L. Saxon
Maureen M. Berner	Diane M. Juffras	Jessica Smith
Mark F. Botts	David M. Lawrence	Karl W. Smith
Joan G. Brannon	Dona G. Lewandowski	Carl W. Stenberg III
Michael Crowell	James M. Markham	John B. Stephens
Shea Riggsbee Denning	Janet Mason	Charles A. Szypszak
James C. Drennan	Laurie L. Mesibov	Shannon H. Tufts
Richard D. Ducker	Christopher B. McLaughlin	Vaughn Upshaw
Robert L. Farb	Kara A. Millonzi	A. John Vogt
Joseph S. Ferrell	Jill D. Moore	Aimee N. Wall
Milton S. Heath Jr.	Jonathan Q. Morgan	Jeffrey B. Welty
Norma Houston (on leave)	Ricardo S. Morse	Richard B. Whisnant
Cheryl Daniels Howell	C. Tyler Mulligan	Gordon P. Whitaker
Jeffrey A. Hughes	David W. Owens	Eileen R. Youens

© 2008
School of Government
The University of North Carolina at Chapel Hill

Use of this publication for commercial purposes or without acknowledgment of its source is prohibited. Reproducing, distributing, or otherwise making available to a non-purchaser the entire publication, or a substantial portion of it, without express permission, is prohibited.
Printed in the United States of America
Cover photo by Daniel Soileau
21 20 19 18 17   2 3 4 5 6
ISBN 978-1-56011-566-3

Summary of Contents

Table of Contents

IV   Discontinuing Utility Services   51

VI Miscellaneous 89

Appendix 91

Index 131

Introduction

Local governments have significant flexibility in structuring and financing water, wastewater, and solid waste utility services, but most cities and counties provide these services as public enterprises.[1] Cities and counties may finance the cost of public enterprise utility services by "levying taxes, borrowing money, and appropriating any other revenues therefor, and by accepting and administering gifts and grants from any source."[2] In addition to these funding

1. *See* N.C. GEN. STAT. §§ 160A-312 through 160A-328 (hereinafter G.S.); G.S. 153A-274 through 153A-294. Unless otherwise indicated, statutory references to G.S. Chapter 160A apply to cities, towns, and villages (referred to collectively as cities), and references to G.S. Chapter 153A apply to counties. The General Assembly also has authorized counties to establish water and sewer districts (G.S. 162A, Art. 6); counties to define special service districts for water and wastewater services (G.S. 153A, Art. 16); cities to define special service districts for wastewater services (G.S. 160A, Art. 23); counties, or two or more political subdivisions (such as cities, towns, incorporated villages, or sanitary districts), to organize water and sewer authorities (G.S. 162A, Art. 1); any two or more political subdivisions in a county to petition the board of commissioners to create a metropolitan water or sewer district (G.S. 162A, Arts. 4 and 5); and the Commission for Health Services to create a sanitary district to operate sewage collection, treatment, and disposal systems and water supply systems for the purpose of preserving and promoting public health and welfare, without regard for county or municipal boundary lines (G.S. 130A, Art. 2, Pt. 2).

Note that for purposes of this publication, the term *public enterprise* refers to the statutory authority for a local government to provide water, wastewater, and solid waste services. It is not limited to the services that must be reported in a separate enterprise fund according to generally accepted accounting principles. For example, even though solid waste services often are accounted for in a unit's general fund, such services comprise public enterprise services under state law.

2. G.S. 160A-313; G.S. 153A-276.

sources, local governments are authorized to impose rates, rents, fees, charges, and penalties (referred to collectively as fees) on customers[3] who receive public enterprise utility services.[4] How, though, can local governments properly bill for the utility services provided? Who is liable for the water, wastewater, and solid waste utility fees? What happens when a customer fails to pay his or her bill? What if the local government underbills a customer for the services provided? The following question-and-answer sequence offers legal guidance to local governments in addressing these and other commonly asked questions regarding billing and collecting fees for water, wastewater, and solid waste services.

This guidance is based on interpretations of applicable constitutional and statutory provisions, supplemented by a wide body of case law from North Carolina and other jurisdictions that has been developed over the course of many years and is known as common law. The focus of the question and answer series is on billing and collecting fees for water, wastewater, and solid waste utility services provided by local governments as public enterprises (referred to collectively as public enterprise utility services).[5] Where indicated, however, the constitutional and statutory provisions and common law principles discussed apply to other public enterprise services provided by cities and counties,[6] as well as to water and wastewater services provided by other government entities such as water and sewer authorities, county water and sewer districts, and

3. For purposes of this publication, unless otherwise indicated, the terms *customer, account holder,* and *contracting party* are used interchangeably and refer to the individual or entity liable for payment of the public enterprise utility service fees. The terms do not necessarily refer to the owner of the property or premises served.

4. G.S. 160A-314; G.S. 153A-277. Likewise, the General Assembly has authorized water and sewer authorities (G.S. 162A-9), county water and sewer districts (G.S. 162A-88), metropolitan water districts (G.S. 162A-49), and metropolitan sewer districts (G.S. 162A-72) to assess rates, fees, and charges for the provision of utility services.

5. Under the public enterprise statutes, *water services* are defined as "water supply and distribution systems"; *wastewater services* are defined as "wastewater collection, treatment, and disposal systems of all types, including septic tank systems or other on-site collection or disposal facilities or systems"; and *solid waste services* are defined as "solid waste collection and disposal systems and facilities." G.S. 160A-311; G.S. 153A-274.

6. Other authorized public enterprise services for cities and counties are airports, off-street parking facilities, public transportation systems, and stormwater management systems. G.S. 160A-311; G.S. 153A-274. Cities additionally are authorized to own and operate electric power systems, natural gas systems, and cable television systems as public enterprises. G.S. 160A-311.

metropolitan water or sewer districts. Relevant constitutional and statutory citations are listed in the text; additional information, including case law citations, is provided in the footnotes.

It is important to note that some of the questions discussed are not susceptible to definitive resolution. To the extent that there are ambiguities, local government officials should discuss the potential consequences of various courses of action with counsel. Furthermore, local officials should be aware that political, strategic, and practical factors also will influence a unit's billing and collecting policies. The legal framework set forth below provides some flexibility for local governments to tailor policies to their needs based on these additional considerations.

1 Establishing a Utility Account

1. May a local government require a potential customer to provide government-issued identification as a condition of establishing an account for public enterprise utility services?

Yes. A city or county has broad authority to "adopt adequate and reasonable rules to protect and regulate a public enterprise belonging to or operated by it." The rules must be adopted by ordinance and applied uniformly to all customers. G.S. 160A-312(b); G.S. 153A-275(b). This authority likely extends to requiring potential customers to provide government-issued identification and other identifying information such as proof of address. A local government, however, must be careful not to engage in unlawful discrimination. To this end, it should allow multiple forms of government-issued identification (such as drivers' licenses, state identification cards, military identifications, and passports) or proof of address (such as utility bills, cable television bills, telephone bills, deeds, and rental agreements).

Note: If a local government collects certain identifying information, it must make sure that the information is kept private. A local government is prohibited from intentionally communicating or otherwise making available to the general public certain identifying information, including Social Security or employer taxpayer identification numbers; driver's license, state identification card, or passport numbers; checking or savings account numbers; credit or debit card numbers; digital signatures; personal identification code (PIN) numbers; biometric data (such as eye scans, voice scans, and DNA); fingerprints; or passwords.[1] G.S. 132-1.10(b)(5).

1. There are several exceptions to the requirement that the identifying information be kept confidential. The requirement does not apply if the identifying information is sufficiently redacted. G.S. 132-1.10(c)(4). Furthermore, a local government may disclose Social Security numbers or other identifying information to another governmental entity or its agents, employees, or contractors if disclosure is necessary for the receiving entity to

2. May a local government require a potential customer to provide a Social Security number as a condition of establishing an account for public enterprise utility services?

No. A local government is permitted to request that a potential customer provide a Social Security number but, under parallel provisions of the Federal Privacy Act, 5 U.S.C. § 552a (note),[2] and the State Privacy Act, G.S. 143-64.60, it cannot deny public enterprise utility services because the potential customer refuses to divulge his or her Social Security number. Furthermore, a local government must inform a potential customer in writing that disclosure of the Social Security number is voluntary and must state the legal authority under which the number is solicited and what uses will be made of the

---

perform its duties and responsibilities. G.S. 132-1.10(c)(1). (If a local government wishes to so disclose a Social Security number, it must inform the customer of the potential disclosure when the Social Security number is collected. 5 U.S.C. § 552a (note) (2007); G.S. 143-64.60.) The receiving party must maintain the confidential status of the information. A local government also may disclose the information if required by a court order, warrant, or subpoena, G.S. 132-1.10(c)(2), or to serve public health purposes in compliance with G.S. 130A. G.S. 132-1.10(c)(3). It may disclose any recorded document in the official records of the register of deeds of the county, G.S. 132-1.10(c)(6), and any document filed in the official records of the courts, G.S. 132-1.10(c)(7).

2. Section 7 of The Privacy Act of 1974, Pub. L. No. 93-579, 5 U.S.C. § 552a (note) (2007), provides that

> (a)(1) It shall be unlawful for any Federal, State or local government agency to deny to any individual any right, benefit, or privilege provided by law because of such individual's refusal to disclose his social security account number.
>
> (2) The provisions of paragraph (1) of this subsection shall not apply with respect to—
>
> > (A) any disclosure which is required by Federal statute, or
> >
> > (B) the disclosure of a social security number to any Federal, State, or local agency maintaining a system of records in existence and operating before January 1, 1975, if such disclosure was required under statute or regulation adopted prior to such date to verify the identity of an individual.
>
> (b) Any Federal, State, or local government agency which requests an individual to disclose his social security account number shall inform that individual whether that disclosure is mandatory or voluntary, by what statutory or other authority such number is solicited, and what uses will be made of it.

See also Yaeger v. Hackensack Water Co., 615 F. Supp. 1087 (D.N.J. 1985) (holding that water company, functioning as state actor, could not obtain a customer's Social Security number except in compliance with the Privacy Act).

number. 5 U.S.C. § 552a (note); G.S. 143-64.60(b); *see also* G.S. 132-1.10(b). A local government must provide enough information about the potential consequences of divulging the Social Security number to allow an individual to make a reasoned choice as to disclosure.[3] The local government is prohibited from using the number for any purpose other than the purposes clearly stated when the number is solicited. G.S. 132-1.10(b)(4).

Note: If the local government collects a Social Security number, there are a number of limitations on its retention and dissemination. See 5 U.S.C. § 552a (note) (2007); G.S. 143-64.60; G.S. 132-1.10(b) and (c). For example, a local government is prohibited from printing an individual's Social Security number on any materials that are mailed to the individual, even if the materials are contained within a sealed envelope. G.S. 132-1.10(b)(9).

3. May a local government require a potential customer to pay a deposit or security fee before providing public enterprise utility services?

Yes. A local government has broad authority to establish "rents, rates, fees, charges, and penalties for the use of or the services furnished by a public enterprise." G.S. 153A-277; G.S. 160A-314. This rate-making authority likely extends to establishing a deposit or security fee requirement for the use of public enterprise utility services.[4]

The deposit or security fee must be reasonable and nondiscriminatory. There is no specific definition of what constitutes a reasonable fee, but generally the deposit or security fee should approximate the risk of loss to the local government in the event of default. For example, it likely is reasonable for a local government to require a deposit or security fee in the amount of the average of one or two months of utility charges per customer for the class of customer requesting service. The deposit or security fee also could be based on the average amount of delinquent funds per customer in the event of default.

3. *See* Am. Fed'n of State, County, and Mun. Employees, Council 75 v. City of Albany 725 P.2d 381 (Or. App. 1986).

4. Other entities likely also are authorized to assess deposit or security fees. *See* G.S. 162A-88 (water and sewer districts); G.S. 162A-49 (metropolitan water districts); G.S. 162A-72 (metropolitan sewer districts). In fact, water and sewer authorities have specific authority to impose deposit fees. G.S. 162A-9.

4. May a local government assess different public enterprise utility service deposit or security fees for different customers?

Yes. A local government may establish a different schedule of deposit or security fees for different classes of customers, or charge the fees to some customers and not to others, as long as the deposit or security fee requirements are reasonable, nondiscriminatory, and consistently enforced.[5] A local government also may charge deposit or security fees, or higher deposit or security fees, to nonresident customers than it charges to resident customers.[6] G.S. 153A-277(a); G.S. 160A-314(a).

With respect to resident customers, a local government should have a rational basis for charging different deposit or security fees to different classes of customers. For example, a local government can charge a higher deposit fee to commercial or industrial customers than to residential customers. It also may charge a higher fee to customers who do not own the property or premises being served or to customers who have a history of delinquent enterprise bill payments or bad credit.[7] Deposit or security fee classifications, however, cannot vary according to ability to pay, disability, or senior citizen status.[8] And, of course, the classifications cannot be based on prohibited grounds such as race, color, alienage, religion, national origin, or gender.

5. Counties and cities have explicit authority to charge different fees for different classes of customers. G.S. 153A-277(a); G.S. 160A-314. Local units may classify customers based on differences in the costs of providing the utility service, as well as differences in "the purpose for which the service or the product is received, the quantity or the amount received, the different character of the service furnished, the time of its use or any other matter which presents a substantial ground of distinction." Wall v. City of Durham, 41 N.C. App. 649, 659, 255 S.E.2d 739, 745 (1979). Other entities providing utility services, such as water and sewer districts, metropolitan districts, and authorities, likely also can establish different classes of customers pursuant to common law authority.

6. See Kara A. Millonzi, *Lawful Discrimination in Utility Ratemaking; Part 2: Classifying Extraterritorial Customers*, Local Finance Bulletin 34 (Oct. 2006). By local act, the City of Asheville is required to charge the same rate to nonresident customers who reside in Buncombe County as it charges its resident customers. See S.L. 2005-140; City of Asheville v. State, 2008 WL 3834026 (N.C. App. Aug. 19, 2008).

7. See, e.g., Washington Gas Light Co. v. Pub. Serv. Comm'n of the District of Columbia, 334 F. Supp. 1062 (D.D.C. 1972).

8. See Kara A. Millonzi, *Lawful Discrimination in Utility Ratemaking; Part 1: Classifying Customers within Territorial Boundaries*, Local Finance Bulletin 33, at 6 (Oct. 2006).

5. May a local government require a deposit or security fee, or a larger deposit or security fee, if a potential public enterprise utility services customer refuses to provide government-issued identification?

Yes. A local government may charge a deposit or security fee, or a larger deposit or security fee, to a customer who refuses to provide proof of identity or proof of address. Any deposit or security fee requirement must be reasonable and nondiscriminatory.[9]

6. May a local government require a deposit or security fee, or a higher deposit or security fee, if a potential public enterprise utility services customer refuses to provide a Social Security number?

Likely yes. Under parallel provisions of the Federal Privacy Act, 5 U.S.C. § 552a (note) (2007), and the State Privacy Act, G.S. 143-64.60, a local government may not deny utility services because a potential customer refuses to divulge his or her Social Security number. A local government, however, probably may charge a deposit or security fee, or a higher deposit or security fee, to a customer who refuses to provide a Social Security number, because making access to utility services more costly to a customer who refuses to provide a Social Security number does not deny the customer access to the utility services per se. If the fee is set too high, though, such a policy might be open to a claim by an individual that he or she effectively is denied services because of inability to pay the deposit or security fee. There currently is no case law addressing this issue.

7. Is a local government required to pay interest to a customer on funds held as a deposit or security fee for public enterprise utility services?

No. There is no legal requirement that a local government pay interest on funds held as a utility deposit.[10] As a matter of practice, a local government may wish to inform a customer at the time the deposit or security fee is tendered that it is non–interest bearing.

9. See Questions 3 and 4.
10. *See* Stephen Holt, *Who is Entitled to Interest Earned by Local Governments?*, LOCAL FINANCE BULLETIN 26 (Nov. 1982).

8. Is a local government required to segregate moneys held as a deposit or security fee for public enterprise utility services?

No. All moneys held by a local government are subject to the provisions of the Local Government Budget and Fiscal Control Act (LGBFCA) (G.S. 159-1 through G.S. 159-42). The LGBFCA requires that all moneys received by a local government be deposited in an official depository.[11] G.S. 159-32. It does not prescribe that moneys received for separate purposes be segregated into different bank accounts.

For accounting and financial reporting purposes, though, a local government should show moneys held as deposits or security fees as a liability in the enterprise fund or general fund, depending on how the other public enterprise utility expenditures and revenues are reported.

9. May a local government refuse to reconnect a public enterprise utility service or establish a new account for service because the individual or entity seeking service is delinquent on payments for service provided at the same property or premises?

Yes. If a public enterprise utility service is discontinued because of a delinquent account, a local government may refuse to reconnect the service or establish a new account with the same customer at the same property or premises until the delinquent amounts, including all penalties, are paid in full.[12]

10. May a local government refuse to reconnect a public enterprise utility service or establish a new account for service because the individual or entity seeking service is delinquent on payments for service provided at a different property or premises?

Maybe. Although there is no North Carolina case law on point, several courts that have addressed this issue hold that a utility does not have common law authority to cut off or refuse service to a customer at one property or premises for failure to pay for utility service furnished at a different location under a

---

11. County water and sewer districts, metropolitan water and sewer districts, sanitary districts, and water and sewer authorities also are subject to the LGBFCA.

12. See Questions 10 and 62.

separate contract.[13] The reasoning is that a utility is obligated to collect moneys owed in the usual way in which debts are collectible and cannot force payment by refusing service under a new contract.

Not all cases are in accord. A few courts have sustained the right of a utility to discontinue or refuse service because of nonpayment of fees for service at a different property or premises, without regard to any statutory, regulatory, or contract provisions.[14] Other courts have upheld refusal of service at an address

---

13. *See, e.g.,* Merrill v. Livermore Falls Light & Power Co., 105 A. 120 (Me. 1918) (holding that a utility cannot refuse to supply a consumer merely because he or she refuses to pay an overdue bill for service at some location other than that for which he or she is demanding a supply); Miller v. Roswell Gas & Elec. Co., 166 P. 1177 (N.M. 1917) ("The authorities are uniform to the effect that a refusal to furnish water or light cannot be sustained merely because the consumer declines and refused to pay for past-due service for some other and independent use, or at some other place or residence."); Hatch v. Consumers' Co., 104 Pac. 670 (Idaho 1909), *aff'd on other grounds,* 224 U.S. 148 ("A water company cannot enforce a rule requiring a consumer to pay an old or disputed bill for water furnished him at some previous time, or some other and independent use, or at some other place or residence, or for a separate or distinct transaction from that for which he is claiming and demanding a water supply, as a condition precedent to supplying him with water, where he tenders payment of the established water rate in advance for the service he is demanding."); *cf.* Komisarek v. New England Tel. & Tel. Co., 282 A.2d 671 (N.H. 1971) (holding that if a utility company intended to assert the right to terminate any service other than that for which the delinquent payment was due, "it was incumbent upon it to make this plain to its consumers by its tariff"); Benson v. Paris Mountain Water Co., 70 S.E. 897 (S.C. 1910) (holding that a water company had no right to cut off the water from a consumer at one place to which it was supplied under contract for refusal of such consumer to pay a bill for water furnished him at another time and place, under another contract); Elwell v. Atlanta Gas Light Co., 181 S.E. 599 (Ga. Ct. App. 1935) (observing that although a utility company has the right to require a reasonable deposit as security for the payment of service to be rendered, it may not refuse service to a consumer merely because he or she declines or refuses to pay a bill for past service rendered at some other place); Gas-Light Co. of Baltimore v. Colliday, 1866 WL 2012 (Md. Ct. App. May 10, 1866) ("[W]here several contracts are made between the same parties for different pieces of property, each requiring its own meter, as in this case, a failure to comply with any terms in relation to one, furnished no excuse or ground to the company to withhold the gas from the other.").

14. *See* Mackin v. Portland Gas Co., 61 P. 134 (Ore. 1900) (holding that the gas company's rule that, in the event of a default, the company could continue the supply of gas until payment is made authorized the gas company to discontinue service to a customer "at one set of premises until payment should be made of [the] delinquent bill for gas furnished him at another" premises).

other than that at which the overdue charges were incurred where the contract employed by the particular utility in its transactions with customers specifically stated that it could deny service for the nonpayment of charges arising "under this contract or any other contract."[15]

It is unclear how North Carolina courts would rule on this issue. If a local government wishes to refuse to provide a public enterprise utility service at a new property or premises because of a delinquency at a previous property or premises, it should, at a minimum, adopt an ordinance stating that it will furnish utility services only to a customer who is not currently delinquent on public enterprise utility services payments owed to the unit.[16] A local government also should consider including language in its contractual agreements with customers warning that future public enterprise utility services may be denied to the customer at any property or premises on account of an outstanding delinquency. It is strongly recommended that a local government consult with its local counsel before adopting such a policy.

Note that instead of denying new service to the customer, the local government may charge a deposit or security fee, or a higher deposit or security fee, because of the outstanding delinquency.[17]

---

15. DePass v. Broad River Power Co., 176 S.E. 325 (S.C. 1934); *see also* Clark v. Utica Gas & Electric Co., 224 A.D. 448 (N.Y. App. Div. 1928) (holding that statutory provision providing that any person who should "neglect or refuse to pay the rent or remuneration due for the same" justified an electric company's termination of service to a customer's current residence because of his refusal to pay an overdue bill for electricity supplied at his previous residence). *But see* Meridian L. & R. Co. v. Steele, 83 So. 414 (Miss. 1919) (holding that a provision in a contract specifying that a utility could discontinue service for the nonpayment of charges incurred "upon such premises or elsewhere" was without consideration insofar as it gave the utility the right to refuse service at the location covered thereby until the customer paid an overdue bill for service rendered at an earlier address).

16. Cities and counties have authority to "protect and regulate any public enterprise system belonging to or operated by [the unit] by adequate and reasonable rules. The rules shall be adopted by ordinance, shall apply to the public enterprise systems both within and outside the [unit's territorial boundaries], and may be enforced with the remedies available under any provision of law." G.S. 160A-312(b); G.S. 153A-275(b).

17. See Question 4.

11. May a local government refuse to establish a new account for public enterprise utility services to an individual or entity seeking service if another individual or entity is delinquent on public enterprise utility fee payments for service provided at the same property or premises?

It depends, in part, on whether the customer who is delinquent on the public enterprise utility service fee payments is the owner of the property or premises.

If the *delinquent customer does not own the property or premises*, the answer generally is no. Under North Carolina law, fees for public enterprise utility services are the legal obligations of the person contracting for them, G.S. 153A-277(c); G.S. 160A-314(c), and "the payment of the delinquent account may not be required before providing services at the request of a new and different tenant or occupant of the premises." G.S. 153A-277(b); G.S. 160A-314(b).

Moreover, under the common law, in the absence of statutory authority to the contrary, liability for payment for public utility services is based on usual contract law. Although utility services may be provided at a particular property or premises, it is the contracting party who is legally liable, on the basis of an express (or possibly implied) contract, for payment of services rendered. To require an applicant to pay a debt for which the applicant is not legally liable has been held to be an impermissible condition on the receipt of utility services.[18]

18. *See* Cascade Motor Hotel, Inc. v. City of Duluth, 348 N.W.2d 84 (Minn. 1984) (holding that because the business relationship between a utility and its customers is rooted in contract, in the absence of a lien or contract, a utility may not impose an obligation of payment for utility services on someone other than the one who actually incurred the debt); Williams v. City of Mount Dora, 452 So. 2d 1143 (Fla. Dist. Ct. App. 1984) (holding that a municipality could not refuse to supply utility service to a customer until the delinquent bill for services supplied to the premises was paid because the potential customer was not legally liable on the delinquent account of the previous owner); *see also* Haynsworth v. South Carolina Elec. & Gas Co., 488 F. Supp. 565 (D.S.C. 1979) (noting that if an "applicant is refused a new account because of past utility services rendered to the dwelling that were made while the applicant was not residing there and for which the applicant is not responsible . . . [it] may run afoul of the Fourteenth Amendment").

A few courts in other jurisdictions have allowed a local government to refuse to provide utility services to a property or premises if the local government can establish that there is some legal relationship between the delinquent account holder and the individual requesting service at the same property or premises, and the individual requesting service benefited from the original provision of service. For example, if the old and new customers are married or have a legal partnership, a local government may refuse to provide service to the new customer at the same property or premises because of the delinquency owed by the old customer.[19]

If the *delinquent customer is the owner of the property or premises*, the answer is less clear. The public enterprise statutes state that "[i]f a delinquent customer is not the owner of the premises to which the services are delivered, the payment of the delinquent account may not be required before providing services at the request of a new and different tenant or occupant of the premises." G.S. 160A-314(b); G.S. 153A-277(b). The provisions imply that if the owner of the property or premises established the account for public enterprise utility services, a local government may refuse to provide services until the delinquent amounts are paid in full, even if the property is occupied by one or more tenants. It also at least suggests that if the owner of a property or premises is delinquent on public enterprise utility payments and sells the property or premises to a new owner, a local government may refuse to provide services until the delinquent amounts are paid in full. (Although in neither case may the local government require that the new tenant, occupant, or owner actually pay the delinquent fees.)

Several federal circuit courts in other jurisdictions, however, have held that refusing to provide services to a tenant, occupant, or new owner of a property or premises because the owner of the property or premises owes delinquent fees

---

19. *See, e.g.*, Haynsworth v. South Carolina Elec. & Gas Co., 488 F. Supp. 565 (D.S.C. 1979) (noting that utility's refusal to allow wife to open new account in her name because there existed an outstanding balance in an account for the same premises in her husband's name was not improper); Williams v. City of Mount Dora, 452 So. 2d 1143 (Fla. Dist. Ct. App. 1984) (noting that if a local government-owned utility could prove that the new customer and the previous customer were legally connected, through a partnership agreement or marriage, or that the new customer had actually benefited from the previous services provided, it may have been able to refuse service to the new customer until the delinquent account was paid).

violates the equal protection clause of the U.S. Constitution.[20] Their reasoning is that such a policy creates two classes of applicants for public enterprise utility services with no rational basis for the distinction. In the first class are applicants for utility services who are not indebted to the local government for utility service fees. The second class includes applicants for utility services who, likewise, are not indebted to the local government for utility service fees but who own or occupy a property or premises where an outstanding debt is owed by a third party. According to the courts, "a collection scheme that divorces itself entirely from the reality of legal accountability for the debt involved is devoid of logical relation to the collection of unpaid water bills from the defaulting debtor."[21] At least one circuit court has rejected this rationale, though, concluding that it unnecessarily restricts the characterization of the local government's interest as not merely the collection of unpaid fees, but the collection of those fees from the defaulting debtor.[22] Instead, the court held that a local government could deny service to a new customer if a previous customer owed delinquent payments for utility services provided at the same property or premises, because there is a rational relationship between such a scheme and the general goal of collecting debts. The Fourth Circuit has not yet addressed this issue; likewise it has not been addressed by North Carolina courts.

Note: Nothing prohibits a local government from adopting a policy whereby it requires property owners to establish any accounts for public enterprise utility services.[23] Such a policy cannot have retroactive application, though.

20. *See* Golden v. City of Columbus, 404 F.3d 950 (6th Cir. 2005); Craft v. Memphis Light, Gas & Water Div., 534 F.2d 684 (6th Cir. 1976), *aff'd on other grounds*, 436 U.S. 1 (1978); Davis v. Weir, 497 F.2d 139 (5th Cir. 1974); *see also* Midkiff v. Adams County Regional Water District, 409 F.3d 758 (6th Cir. 2005) (noting that it violates equal protection to treat tenants whose landlords owe a local government payment for utility services differently than tenants whose landlords do not have such a debt); O'Neal v. City of Seattle, 66 F.3d 1064 (9th Cir. 1995) (stating that refusing a new tenant water service because of the debt of an unrelated prior customer is illogical).

21. *See, e.g.*, Sterling v. Village of Maywood, 579 F.2d 1350, 1355 (7th Cir. 1978) (concluding that "refusal to reinstate water service because the landlord has failed to pay the water bill is a violation of the tenant's right to equal protection").

22. Ransom v. Marrazzo, 848 F.2d 398 (3d Cir. 1988).

23. See Question 13.

12. May a local government refuse to establish a new account for public enterprise utility services if the property or premises to be served fails to meet required building codes or is otherwise uninhabitable?

No, unless the condition of the property or premises directly affects the provision of public enterprise utility services. In *Dale v. City of Morganton*,[24] the North Carolina Supreme Court stated that a local government

> may not deprive an inhabitant, otherwise entitled thereto, of light, water or other utility service as a means of compelling obedience to its police regulations, however valid and otherwise enforceable those regulations may be. The right of a [local government] to cut off or refuse a service rendered by it in its proprietary capacity must be determined as if the [local government], in its capacity of supplier of such service, were a person separate and apart from the city as a unit of government.[25]

The court, however, recognized that because a local government engaged in the proprietary function of supplying utility service to customers is liable for injuries due to its negligence, it could, in order to obviate possible future liability, refuse to render service to a customer when inspection of the customer's property or premises revealed that provision of the utility service would present a dangerous condition.

13. May a local government require the owner of a property or premises to establish the account for public enterprise utility services?

Yes. There are no constitutional, statutory, or common law provisions prohibiting a local government from requiring the owner of the property or premises to be the contracting party for purposes of establishing an account and being

---

24. 270 N.C. 567, 155 S.E.2d 136 (1967).

25. *Id.* at 572–73, 155 S.E.2d at 142 (holding that city could not deny electric service to a building in order to compel obedience to its decree forbidding use of the building for human habitation); *see also* Am. Jur. 2d Public Utilities § 18 (noting that the decisions are generally in accord in holding that a utility cannot refuse to render the service that it is authorized to furnish because of some collateral matter not related to that service).

liable for public enterprise utility service payments.[26] A local unit may require a potential customer to submit proof of ownership of the property or premises to be served, such as a copy of a deed of trust.

But, even if the owner of the property is the contracting party or otherwise legally liable to pay the utility fees, a local government generally may not place a lien on the property served. G.S. 153A-277(c); G.S. 160A-314(c). There is one exception to this general rule. A local government may choose to bill for solid waste services on the property tax bill, as opposed to billing for solid waste services along with other enterprise services.[27] If the local government includes the fees for solid waste services on the property tax bill and adopts an ordinance that states that delinquent fees may be collected in the same manner as delinquent real property taxes, the solid waste fees are a lien on the real property described on the bill that includes the fee. G.S. 153A-293; G.S. 160A-314.1(b).

14. If a local government requires the owner of one property to be the contracting party for public enterprise utility services, must it require the owners of all properties to be the contracting parties?

No. If a local government requires the owner of one property to be the contracting party, it does not have to require the owners of all properties to be the contracting parties for purposes of establishing a public enterprise utility service account. A city or county, for instance, likely could establish a criterion that after "X" number of defaults on utility fee payments at a rental property or premises, the owner of the property or premises will be required to be the contracting party.

26. *See generally* Midkiff v. Adams County Reg'l Water Dist., 409 F.3d 758 (6th Cir. 2005) (holding that water district's policy of contracting only with property owners did not violate equal protection); Puckett v. City of Muldraugh, 403 S.W.2d 252 (Ky. Ct. App. 1966) (holding that ordinance that stated that "the rates and charges [for utility services] shall be billed to the owner of the premises except that upon application by the tenant of any premises, who is not the owner thereof, filed with the Board of Trustees of said city, an application to have water and sewer services rendered to said tenant, renter, or party occupying premises" was not arbitrary or unreasonable). A local government, however, may not require the owner of the property to pay debts and fees owed by a prior contracting party for services provided at the property or premises.

27. See Question 17.

Because the utility is a state actor, it is subject to the requirements of the equal protection clauses of the United States and North Carolina constitutions. Thus the utility must have a rational basis for requiring owners to be the contracting parties in some instances while allowing nonowners to be the contracting parties in other instances. If a local government requires one or more owners to be the contracting parties, it should do so according to a consistent policy and not on an ad hoc basis. And, of course, classifications cannot be based on prohibited grounds such as race, color, alienage, religion, national origin, or gender.

15. Does a local government have to provide public enterprise utility services to any applicant who applies for service?

Generally no. With the exception of certain provisions governing involuntary annexations,[28] a local government does not have a legal duty to extend public enterprise utility services to every property within its territorial borders (or to extraterritorial property). In fact, a local government has no obligation to provide public enterprise utility services to any of its citizens. Once a city or county chooses to provide services, however, it must base its decisions about whom to provide the services on valid, utility-based considerations, such as the cost of providing the services and existing and future capacity needs. A unit may not make determinations on an ad hoc basis or deny service based on prohibited grounds such as race, color, alienage, religion, national origin, or gender. A local government should develop and follow a uniform plan setting forth the circumstances under which it will provide public enterprise utility services.

16. May a local government require a property owner or occupant to use the local government's *water* and *wastewater* services?

No. A local government may not require a property owner or occupant to use its water or wastewater services, but it can approximate the same result by assessing an availability fee under some circumstances. A local government may require the owner of certain developed property that is located within

---

28. *See* 2 David M. Lawrence, Annexation Law in North Carolina: Voluntary Annexation § 6.02 (2004).

its territorial limits to connect to the water or sewer line or both.[29] In lieu of requiring connection, a local government may assess a periodic availability charge, as long as the fee does not exceed the minimum periodic service charge for properties that are connected. G.S. 160A-317; G.S. 153A-284. The property must contain at least one residential dwelling unit or commercial establishment and must be located within a reasonable distance of any water line or wastewater collection line owned, leased, or operated by the local government or on behalf of the local government.[30]

If a property owner connects to the water or sewer line, a local government cannot require the property owner to actually use the local government's water or wastewater services.[31] And, once a property is connected, a local government likely cannot charge the periodic availability fee.[32] It can structure its fee schedule and contractual agreements, however, so as to assess a minimum monthly service charge even at a zero consumption level.

17. May a local government require a property owner to use the unit's *solid waste disposal or collection* services?

It depends on both the nature of the solid waste services and the type of local government.

Solid waste disposal services. Neither a county nor a city may require a property owner or occupant to use its solid waste disposal services, but it may approximate the same result by assessing an availability fee under certain circumstances. A local government may impose a fee for the availability of any disposal facilities that it provides. The fee for availability may be imposed

---

29. The definition of *wastewater services* under the public enterprise statutes includes septic tank systems (*see* G.S. 153A-274(2); G.S. 160A-311(3)), but a local government likely does not have the authority to require property owners to submit to required septic system inspections or a septic system management program under its public enterprise authority. A local government, however, may be able to require septic system inspections and charge a reasonable fee to cover the costs of the inspections pursuant to its regulatory powers. *See generally* Homebuilders Ass'n of Charlotte, Inc. v. City of Charlotte, 336 N.C. 37, 442 S.E.2d 45 (1994).

30. A local government does not have the authority to require property in industrial use to connect to its water or wastewater systems.

31. Note, however, that certain cross-connections are prohibited by state regulations.

32. See Question 38.

on all "improved property" within the local government's territorial borders that benefits from the availability of the disposal facilities. The statutes do not define *improved property*, but it likely requires that there be a residential, commercial, or industrial structure on the real property. The fee, however, may not exceed the cost of providing the local government's disposal facilities.[33] G.S. 160A-314.1; G.S. 153A-292.

Furthermore, a local government "may not impose an availability fee on property whose solid waste is collected by a county, a city, or a private contractor for a fee if the fee imposed by a county, a city, or a private contractor for the collection of solid waste includes a charge for the availability and use of a disposal facility provided by the county." G.S. 160A-314.1; G.S. 153A-292. Additionally, "[p]roperty served by a private contractor who disposes of solid waste collected from the property in a disposal facility provided by a private contractor that provides the same services as those provided by the city disposal facility is not considered to benefit from a disposal facility" provided by the local government and is not subject to the availability fee. G.S. 160A-314.1; G.S. 153A-292. If the services provided at the private contractor's disposal facility are not coextensive with those provided by the local government, the unit may assess an availability fee to cover the costs of the additional services. For example, if a private hauler's disposal facility does not provide recycling services but the local government's disposal facilities do, the local government may impose an availability fee on residents served by the private hauler to cover the costs of the recycling services.

Note: A local government may assess an additional fee on individuals or entities that actually use the unit's solid waste disposal facilities. G.S. 160A-314.1; G.S. 153A-292. The fee for the use of a disposal facility provided by a county may not exceed the cost of operating the facility; the same restriction does not apply to a fee assessed for the use of a disposal facility provided by a city.

Solid waste collection services. Although a county is authorized to provide solid waste collection services, it may not require a property owner or occupant to use its collection services. G.S. 153A-292. A city, however, may require all owners of "improved property" within its territorial borders to "[p]articipate in any solid waste collection service provided by the city or by a person who

33. *See* Manning v. County of Halifax, 166 N.C. App. 279, 603 S.E.2d 168 (2004).

has a contract with the city if the owner or occupant of the property has not otherwise contracted for the collection of solid waste from the property." G.S. 160-317(b). The statute does not define *improved property*, but it likely requires that there be a residential, commercial, or industrial structure on the real property. A city also may impose a fee for its solid waste collection services, but the fee may not exceed the costs of collection.

18. What are the federal Red Flag Rules and are local governments that provide public enterprise utility services required to comply with the rules?

In 2007 the Federal Trade Commission (FTC), the federal bank regulatory agencies, and the National Credit Union Administration issued regulations, known as the Red Flag Rules, requiring certain financial institutions and other creditors to develop and implement written identify theft prevention programs to identify, detect, and respond to patterns, practices, or specific activities that could indicate identify theft.[34] The regulations were adopted pursuant to the federal Fair and Accurate Credit Transactions (FACT) Act of 2003.[35] The regulations became effective on November 1, 2008, although the FTC has indicated that it will delay enforcement of the Red Flag Rules until May 1, 2009.[36]

The Red Flag Rules apply to financial institutions or creditors that have covered accounts. A *creditor* is defined as any entity that regularly extends, renews, or continues credit; any entity that regularly arranges for the extension, renewal, or continuation of credit; or any assignee of an original creditor who is involved in the decision to extend, renew, or continue credit. Under this definition, a local government entity that bills customers for public enterprise utility services after the services are provided is a creditor. A *covered account* is either (1) an account used mostly for personal, family, or household purposes that involves multiple payments or transactions, or (2) any other account that the creditor offers or maintains for which there is a reasonably foreseeable risk

34. 16 C.F.R. pt. 681 (2008).

35. Pub. L. No. 108-159, 117 Stat. (2003) 1952 (codified as 15 U.S.C. § 1681m(e) and 15 U.S.C. § 1681c(h)).

36. *See* FTC Release, FTC Will Grant Six-Month Delay of Enforcement of 'Red Flags' Rule Requiring Creditors and Financial Institutions to Have Identity Theft Prevention Programs (Oct. 22, 2008), at www.ftc.gov/opa/2008/10/redflags.shtm (last visited Nov. 9, 2008).

to customers from identity theft. A public enterprise utility account constitutes a covered account.

Thus a local government that provides public enterprise utility services and maintains customer accounts is required to comply with the Red Flag Rules. All of the public enterprise utility accounts held by customers of the local unit—whether residential, commercial, or industrial—are covered by the rules.

19. How does a local government that provides public enterprise utility services comply with the Red Flag Rules?

A local government must develop and maintain a governing board–approved, written Identity Theft Prevention Program (ITP Program) that is designed to detect, prevent, and mitigate identity theft in connection with the opening and maintaining of a covered account.[37] *Identity theft* is defined as "fraud committed using the identifying information of another person." *Identifying information* includes "any name or number that may be used, alone or in conjunction with any other information, to identify a specific person." Examples include a name, address, telephone number, Social Security number, date of birth, driver's license number, alien registration number, government passport number, employer or taxpayer identification number, bank routing code, or computer's Internet protocol (IP) address. A local government has flexibility to develop a program that is appropriate to the size and complexity of the unit and the nature and scope of its activities, although the regulations specify the following requirements for the establishment and administration of an ITP Program:

- The ITP Program must be in writing.
- The ITP Program must include reasonable policies and procedures to (1) identify relevant red flags for the covered accounts and incorporate those red flags into the program, (2) detect red flags that have been incorporated into the program, (3) respond appropriately to any red flags that are detected to prevent and mitigate identity theft, and (4) ensure that the program is periodically updated to reflect changes in risks.
- The local government's governing board must approve the initial ITP Program.

37. See Question 18.

- The local government's staff must be trained, as necessary, to effectively implement the ITP Program.
- One or more local government employees or officials must provide administrative oversight of the ITP Program and prepare periodic reports for the governing board.

Identifying red flags. As an initial matter, the regulations require a local government to identify certain *red flags*, defined as patterns, practices, or specific activities that indicate the possible existence of identity theft, in each of five categories. Examples of potential red flags in each of the categories are listed below; however, the list is not exhaustive. (Appendix A to the Red Flag Rules contains additional suggested red flags.[38]) A local government must identify red flags that are relevant to its ITP Program. In so doing, a unit should consider the types of accounts that it offers and maintains, the methods it provides to open and access its accounts, and its previous experiences with identity theft.

1. Notification and Warnings from Credit Reporting Agencies
   - Report of fraud accompanying a credit report
   - Notice or report from a credit agency of a credit freeze on an existing customer or applicant for service
2. Suspicious Documents
   - Identification document or card that appears to be forged, altered, or inauthentic
   - Other document with information that is not consistent with existing customer information, such as a person's signature on a check that appears forged
3. Suspicious Personal Identifying Information
   - Identifying information presented that is inconsistent with other information the customer provides
   - Identifying information presented that is consistent with fraudulent activity, such as an invalid phone number or fictitious billing address
   - Social Security number, address, or phone number that is the same as one given by another customer

---

38. 16 C.F.R. pt. 681 (2008).

4. Suspicious Account Activity or Unusual Use of Account
   - Notice to the local government that an account has unauthorized activity
   - Change of address for an account followed by a request to change the account holder's name
   - Unauthorized access to or use of customer account information
5. Alerts from Others
   - Notice to the local government from a customer, identity theft victim, law enforcement officer, or other person that the unit has opened or is maintaining a fraudulent account

Detecting red flags. Once a local government identifies red flags and incorporates them into its ITP Program, it must implement sufficient policies and procedures to detect those red flags. For example, it may require personnel to take certain steps to obtain and verify the identity of a person opening a public enterprise utility account.[39] Likewise, it may adopt certain procedural requirements to monitor transactions on open accounts, such as verifying the identity of customers who request information and verifying requested changes to an account.

Responding to red flags. It is not enough simply to detect the red flags—a local government must take sufficient steps to respond appropriately to guard against identity theft. A unit's response to individual red flags may vary based on the degree of risk posed and, under some circumstances, no response may be warranted. Appropriate actions by a local government that detects one or more red flags may include, but are not limited to, the following: (1) monitoring the covered account for evidence of identity theft, (2) contacting the customer, (3) changing any passwords associated with the covered account, (4) establishing a new account number for the covered account, (5) closing an existing covered account, (6) refusing to open a new covered account, and (7) notifying law enforcement.

Additionally, a local government should ensure that its internal operating procedures are designed to protect customer identifying information. It should make certain that its website is secure or provide clear notice that it is

---

39. See Questions 1 and 2.

not secure, and it should keep any computer virus protection up to date. A unit also should ensure that office computers are password protected and that offices are clear of papers containing customer information.

Updating the ITP Program. A local government must periodically update its ITP Program to reflect the unit's experiences with identity theft, changes in the type or format of the unit's covered accounts, changes in the methods of identity theft, and changes in the methods to detect, prevent, and mitigate identity theft.

20. May a local government run a credit check on a potential public enterprise utility services customer?

Yes. Under the federal Fair Credit Reporting Act, a local government is authorized to access a credit report of a potential public enterprise utility services customer from one or more consumer reporting agencies.[40]

A local government may vary the amount of a deposit or security fee based on credit scores.[41]

Note: In 2007 the Federal Trade Commission, the federal bank regulatory agencies, and the National Credit Union Administration issued regulations prescribing specific duties for users of consumer reports regarding address discrepancies.[42] The regulations were adopted pursuant to the Federal Fair and Accurate Credit Transactions (FACT) Act of 2003.[43] According to the regulations, a local government must adopt appropriate policies and procedures to verify that a consumer report relates to the individual about whom the unit has requested the report if the local government receives notice from a consumer reporting agency that the address the unit submitted pursuant to a credit check is substantially different from that in the agency's file for the individual.

40. 15 U.S.C. § 1681b (2007).
41. See Question 4.
42. 16 C.F.R. pt. 681 (2008).
43. Pub. L. No. 108-159, 117 Stat. 1952 (2003) (codified as 15 U.S.C. § 1681m(e) and 15 U.S.C. § 1681c(h)).

II Billing for Utility Services Fees

21. May a local government include fees for more than one public enterprise utility service furnished to a property or premises on the same bill?

Yes. A city or county may include fees or charges for any public enterprise services it provides on a single bill. G.S. 160A-314(b); G.S. 153A-277(b). A county is authorized to provide public enterprise services for water, wastewater, solid waste collection and disposal, airports, off-street parking facilities, public transportation systems, and stormwater management programs. G.S. 153A-374. A city is authorized to provide public enterprise services for water, wastewater, electricity, natural gas, public transportation, solid waste collection and disposal, cable television, off-street parking, airports, and stormwater management programs. G.S. 160A-311.

22. Are there any advantages to including more than one public enterprise utility service fee on the same bill?

Yes. Sending a single bill for the various public enterprise utility service charges is more efficient and cost-effective. Moreover, a local government may determine by ordinance the order in which partial payments are to be applied among the various public enterprise services covered by the bill. G.S. 160A-314(b); G.S. 153A-277(b). This allows the local government to apply payments to public enterprise services that are less essential first and disconnect the services that remain unpaid. For example, if a local government provides both water and solid waste collection services, it may include the fees for both services on the same bill and apply partial payments to the solid waste collection services first. Such a policy provides a greater incentive to a customer to pay the public enterprise utility services bill in full to avoid disconnection of water services.

23. Are there any disadvantages to including more than one public enterprise utility service fee on the same bill?

Generally no. One exception may be billing for solid waste services. A local government has the authority to adopt ordinances providing that any fee for solid waste collection or disposal be billed with property taxes. If the ordinance so states, the delinquent fees may be collected in the same manner as delinquent real property taxes, and the fees are a lien on the real property described in the bill that includes the fees.[1] G.S. 160A-314.1(b); G.S. 153A-293. If solid waste collection or disposal fees are billed along with the other enterprise services fees (and all the fees are not included on the property tax bill), the fees are not a lien on the underlying real property. G.S. 160A-314.1(b); G.S. 153A-293.

24. May a local government include other taxes or fees on the bill for public enterprise utility fees?

Yes. There is no legal prohibition against including other local taxes and fees (such as regulatory fees or general user fees) on the bill for public enterprise utility services. A local government, however, may not disconnect its public enterprise utility services for nonpayment of the other taxes and fees.[2]

25. May a local government include fees for public enterprise utility services on the property tax bill?

Yes. A local government has specific authority to include fees for solid waste services on the property tax bill. By local ordinance, a city or county may require that solid waste services fees "be billed with property taxes, [ ] be payable in the same manner as property taxes, and, in the case of nonpayment, [ ] be collected in any manner by which delinquent personal or real property taxes can be collected." G.S. 160A-314.1; G.S. 153A-293.

---

1. See Question 25.
2. G.S. 160A-314 and G.S. 153A-277 authorize cities and counties, respectively, to bill all of their public enterprise utility services on the same bill and to specify the order of partial payments of the public enterprise utility services only so that the more essential services may be disconnected if the entire bill is not paid. The public enterprise utility services are water, sewer, stormwater, electric, natural gas, public transportation, airports, solid waste, cable television, and off-street parking facilities—fees for these services are the only ones that can be grouped together for purposes of disconnecting services for nonpayment.

If a local government chooses to bill for solid waste services on the property tax bill, the fees are a lien on the underlying property served. The lien has the same priority status as a lien for real or personal property taxes; it is superior to all other liens and rights except previously recorded liens for state taxes, regardless of whether the other liens were acquired before the lien for the delinquent fees. G.S. 105-356(a)(1) & (2). Furthermore, once the lien has attached to real property, its priority is not affected by transfer of title, by death, or by receivership of the property owner. G.S. 105-356(a)(3). A local government must follow the procedures set forth in G.S. 105-369, G.S. 105-374, and G.S. 105-375 for enforcement of the lien against the real property. A unit also may employ the remedies of levy and attachment and garnishment against personal property to enforce the collection of delinquent fees.[3] G.S. 105-366; G.S. 105-367; G.S. 105-368.

With respect to other public enterprise utility services, there are no statutory provisions prohibiting including the fees for these services on the property tax bill, but, unlike solid waste services fees, they are not payable or collectible in the same manner as property taxes.[4] Significantly, they are not a lien on the underlying property.

26. May a local government include an individual's Social Security number on the bill for public enterprise utility service?

No. A local government is prohibited from printing an individual's Social Security number on any materials that are mailed to the individual, even if the materials are contained within a sealed envelope. G.S. 132-1.10(b)(9). A local government is permitted to print a Social Security number that has been redacted, though. G.S. 132-1.10(c)(4). Deleting all but the last four digits of the Social Security number likely constitutes a sufficient redaction.

3. For a detailed description of the collection process for delinquent property taxes, see Shea Riggsbee Denning, *The Property Tax, in* County and Municipal Government in North Carolina 19–25 (David M. Lawrence ed., 2006).
4. Several units, particularly those that do not provide water and wastewater services, include a fee for stormwater management services on the property tax bill.

27. May a local government distribute its public enterprise utility services bills in postcard form?

Likely yes, even though distributing public enterprise utility services bills in postcard form potentially exposes the billing information to the public. Generally, billing information "compiled and maintained by a city or county or other public entity providing utility services . . . is not a public record . . . ." G.S. 132-1.1(c). *Billing information* is defined as "any record or information, in whatever form, compiled or maintained with respect to individual customers." The statute provides, however, that nothing in its terms is intended to limit a local government entity from releasing billing information if it is "necessary to assist the city, county, State, or public enterprise to maintain the integrity and quality of services it provides." G.S. 132-1.1(c)(2). If sending bills in postcard form is a more efficient mechanism for billing and collecting utility fee payments, it likely is allowed under the exemption provision.[5] A local government must ensure that it does not improperly disclose a customer's Social Security number[6] or other protected identifying information.[7]

---

5. Note that the statute details two other circumstances in which billing information may be released—in connection with bond financing associated with the public enterprise, and when necessary to assist public safety, emergency management, or judicial officers with their duties. It is likely, however, that a local government can release billing information under circumstances other than those specified in the statute. *See* DAVID M. LAWRENCE, PUBLIC RECORDS LAW FOR NORTH CAROLINA LOCAL GOVERNMENTS 56–58 (Supp. 2004).

6. A local government is prohibited under state law from intentionally communicating or otherwise making available to the general public a person's Social Security number. G.S. 132-1.10(b)(5). Furthermore, it is a felony violation under federal law to disclose any Social Security number or related record that was obtained or maintained by authorized persons pursuant to any provision of law enacted on or after October 1, 1990. 42 U.S.C. § 405(c)(2)(C)(viii) (2007).

7. As discussed in Questions 1 and 2, a local government is prohibited from intentionally communicating or otherwise making available to the general public a person's identifying information, including Social Security or employer taxpayer identification numbers; driver's license, state identification card, or passport numbers; checking or savings account numbers; credit or debit card numbers; digital signatures; personal identification codes; biometric data; fingerprints; or passwords. G.S. 132-1.10(b)(5). The requirement that the identifying information be kept confidential does not apply if the information is sufficiently redacted. G.S. 132-1.10(c)(4).

28. May a local government send its public enterprise utility services bills by the United States Postal Service's Standard Mail delivery?

No. A local government is not required, under state law, to distribute utility bills by First Class mail. In fact, a local government likely may distribute its utility bills in postcard form.[8] The United States Postal Service, however, prescribes certain criteria for mail to qualify for Standard Mail delivery. Standard Mail may not be used for "sending personal correspondence, handwritten or typewritten letters, or bills and statements of account."[9]

29. May a local government contract with a private entity to compile and distribute its public enterprise utility services bills?

Yes. A city or county is authorized to "contract with . . . any person, association, or corporation, in order to carry out any public purpose that the [local government] is authorized by law to engage in." G.S. 153A-449; G.S. 160A-20.1.

Furthermore, a city that operates a wastewater utility, but not a water utility, has explicit authority to contract with the owner or operator of a water distribution system operating within the area served by the city's wastewater utility to act as the billing and collection agent for any fees or penalties imposed by the city for wastewater services.[10] G.S. 160A-315.

30. May a local government contract with another local government in North Carolina to compile and distribute its public enterprise utility services bills?

Yes. North Carolina law authorizes local governments to cooperate in exercising the powers granted to them—"[a]ny unit of local government in this State and any one or more other units of local government . . . may enter into

---

8. See Question 27.

9. www.usps.com/send/waystosendmail/senditwithintheus/standardmail.htm (last visited March 21, 2008).

10. In the alternative, a city that operates a wastewater utility, but not a water utility, may require the owner or operator of any independent or private water distribution system operating within the city to furnish copies of water meter readings and any other consumption records and data that the city may require to bill and collect wastewater fees. G.S. 160A-316.

contracts or agreements with each other in order to execute an undertaking," G.S. 160A-461. An *undertaking* is defined as "the joint exercise by two or more units of local government, or the contractual exercise by one unit for one or more other units, or any power, function, public enterprise, right, privilege, or immunity.[11] G.S. 160A-460(1).

31. Does a local government have to provide specific information on its public enterprise utility services bill?

Maybe. To the extent that a local government is required to provide notice to a customer and an opportunity for the customer to dispute any fees before the unit may discontinue service for nonpayment,[12] the local government likely will have to provide information on consumption levels and rates in order to give the customer sufficient notice of the nature of the fees being charged.[13] Even in the absence of a legal requirement, many local governments choose to provide this information in order to avoid confusing customers and to aid in educating customers about consumption patterns. Several local governments provide additional information on historical use for purposes of comparison.

32. May a local government accept credit cards, debit cards, or other forms of electronic payment for public enterprise utility fees?

Yes. A city or county is authorized to accept *electronic payment*, defined as "payment by charge card, credit card, debit card, or by electronic funds transfer . . . ." for any tax, assessment, rate, fee, charge, interest, or penalty owed.[14] G.S. 159-32.1; G.S. 147-86.20; *see also* G.S. 105-357(b) (applying to solid waste services fees included on the property tax bill).

---

11. *See also* G.S. 153A-278 ("Two or more counties, cities, or other units of local government may cooperate in the exercise of any power granted by [Article 15] according to the procedures and provisions of Chapter 160A, Article 20, Part 1.").

12. See Question 51.

13. See Question 52.

14. County water and sewer districts, metropolitan water and sewer districts, sanitary districts, and water and sewer authorities, likewise, are authorized to accept payment by electronic means. G.S. 159-32.1; G.S. 147-86.20.

33. If a local government allows payment of public enterprise utility fees by credit cards, debit cards, or other electronic means, is the local government authorized to pay the credit card company or financial institution a processing or transaction fee for use of the electronic payment services?

Yes. Under state law, a city or county is authorized to pay "any negotiated discount, processing fee, transaction fee, or other charge imposed by a credit card, charge card, or debit card company, or by a third-party merchant bank, as a condition of contracting for the unit's . . . acceptance of electronic payment." G.S. 159-32.1.

34. If a local government offers more than one payment method (for example by mail, by telephone, by Internet, in person), may it charge an administrative fee to a customer who utilizes a certain payment method?

Yes. A local government may assess an administrative fee if a customer chooses a certain payment method over other possible methods. For example, a local government may charge a fee for paying a public enterprise utility fee over the Internet, even though it does not assess a similar fee for payment by mail or in person. The administrative fee should be nondiscriminatory and reasonable. A reasonable fee likely approximates the additional costs associated with the payment method.

35. If a local government allows payment of public enterprise utility fees by credit cards, debit cards, or other electronic means, may it charge an administrative fee to a customer who uses one of the electronic payment options?

Yes. If allowed by the contractual agreement between a local government and the credit card, charge card, debit card, or banking institution, a local government may impose a surcharge on the amount paid by an individual or entity using electronic payment. G.S. 159-32.1.

Many financial institutions, however, prohibit entities from assessing administrative fees, or passing on processing or transaction charges assessed by the electronic payment institutions, to customers who use one of the electronic payment options. Because of this, local governments often absorb the administrative, processing, or transaction fees assessed by the electronic payment institutions.[15] Alternatively, several local governments have contracted with outside agencies to collect electronic payments over the Internet and remit the proceeds to the local governments. The outside agencies typically assesses a small administrative fee to customers to accept the electronic payments over the Internet but do not charge the local government a fee for providing the service.

15. See Question 33.

III Liability for Utility Services Fees

36. Who is liable for payment of the fees and penalties assessed for *water* and *wastewater* public enterprise utility services provided by a local government?

It depends on the nature of the fees and penalties being assessed. A local government may assess fees and penalties for water and wastewater services actually furnished to a property or premises. A city and county also may impose a fee for the availability of water and wastewater services by the local government on certain developed property.

Fees and penalties assessed for public enterprise water and wastewater services furnished to a property or premises. Generally, the payment of any valid fees and penalties assessed for water and wastewater utility services provided by a local government is the "legal obligation[] of the person contracting for [the services]." G.S. 160A-314(c); G.S. 153A-277(c). Thus the individual or entity that establishes the account and enters into the contractual relationship with the local government for water and wastewater services is responsible for the fees and penalties assessed for the provision of those services. Such fees include deposit fees, monthly fixed fees, variable fees based on consumption, and penalties for nonpayment or penalties assessed for violations of public enterprise utility regulations.

There are two exceptions to the general rule that only the contracting party is liable for water and wastewater fees and penalties. The owner of the property or premises to which the local government provides water or wastewater services is legally obligated to pay any valid fees and penalties, even if the owner is not the contracting party, if (1) the property or premises served is leased or rented to more than one tenant and utility service rendered to more than one tenant is measured by the same meter, or (2) the fees for wastewater utility service are billed separately from the fees for water utility service. G.S. 160A-314(d); G.S. 153A-277(d). Even if one of the exceptions applies, however, the fees are not a lien on the property or premises served. G.S. 160A-314(c); G.S. 153A-277(c).

In addition to the two statutory exceptions, a local government may require another party to enter into a contractual agreement to pay any fees owed in the event of a default by the primary account holder. For example, a local government may require owners of rental property to co-sign the application for a public enterprise utility service, thereby agreeing to be liable for any delinquent fees owed by a tenant. Absent such a written contractual agreement, however, a local government may not transfer legal liability for the fees to another party.

Availability fees and penalties for public enterprise water and wastewater services. A city or county is authorized to require an owner of certain developed property to connect the owner's property with the local government's water or wastewater system, or both.[1] The property must contain at least one residential dwelling unit or commercial establishment and be located within a reasonable distance of any water line or wastewater collection line owned, leased, or operated by the local government or on behalf of the local government. In lieu of requiring the property owner to connect to the water or wastewater lines, a local government may require the payment of a periodic availability fee, as long as the fee does not exceed the minimum periodic service or administrative charge assessed to properties that are connected. G.S. 153A-284; G.S. 160A-317. The owner of the property assessed the availability fee is liable for its payment, regardless of who occupies the property or premises. The availability fee is not a lien on the property or premises served, though. G.S. 160A-314(c); G.S. 153A-277(c).

---

1. A local government does not have the authority to require property in industrial use to connect to its water or wastewater systems.

37. Who is liable for payment of the fees and penalties assessed for *solid waste* public enterprise utility services provided by a local government?

It depends both on the nature of the fees and penalties being assessed and on the method of billing for those fees and penalties. As with water and waste-water utilities, a local government may assess fees for solid waste collection and disposal services furnished to a property or premises. A city or county also may impose a fee for the availability of a disposal facility provided by the local government on all improved property that benefits from the availability of the facility. A city or county has two options for billing for solid waste fees and penalties—it may bill for the solid waste fees along with the fees for other enterprise services provided by the local government, or it may include the fees for solid waste services on the property tax bill.[2]

Fees and penalties assessed for public enterprise solid waste services furnished to a property or premises and billed with the fees for other enterprise services. Generally, the payment of any valid fees and penalties assessed for solid waste services provided by a local government is the "legal obligation [ ] of the person contracting for [the services]." G.S. 160A-314(c); G.S. 153A-277(c). Thus the individual or entity that establishes the account and enters into the contractual relationship with the local government for solid waste collection or disposal services is responsible for payment of any fees and penalties assessed for the provision of those services. Such fees include deposit fees, monthly fixed fees, variable fees based on consumption, and penalties for nonpayment or penalties assessed for violations of public enterprise utility regulations.

A local government, however, may require another party to enter into a contractual agreement to pay any fees owed in the event of a default by the primary account holder. For example, a local government may require owners of rental property to co-sign the application for a public enterprise utility service, thereby agreeing to be liable for any delinquent fees owed by a tenant. Absent such a written contractual agreement, however, a local government may not transfer legal liability for the fees to another party.

---

2. A city or county also may contract with another local government or private entity to bill for the fees. *See* G.S. 160A-20.1; G.S. 153A-449.

Fees and penalties assessed for public enterprise solid waste services furnished to a property or premises and billed on the property tax bill. In addition to billing for solid waste services along with other enterprise services, a local government is authorized to adopt an ordinance providing that any fees and penalties for collecting or disposing of solid waste may be included on the property tax bill and payable in the same manner as property taxes.[3] If a local government bills for solid waste services on the property tax bill, any delinquent fees may be collected in the same manner by which delinquent personal or real property taxes are collected. G.S. 160A-314.1(b); G.S. 153A-293. The fees are the liability of the owner of the property or premises served, regardless of who occupies the property or premises. Moreover, the fees are a lien on the real property described on the bill that includes the fees. The lien attaches on the date as of which the real property is to be listed under G.S. 105-285.[4]

The statutory language authorizing solid waste fees to be "payable in the same manner as property taxes" authorizes a local government to bill for the services in advance, G.S. 105-347, and allows the unit to provide a discount for prepayment and impose statutory interest penalties for delinquent payments, G.S. 105-360. Moreover, the language authorizing delinquent solid waste fees to be "collected in the same manner by which delinquent personal or real property taxes are collected" authorizes a local government to enforce the lien against the real property according to the procedures set forth in G.S. 105-356, G.S. 105-369, G.S. 105-374, and G.S. 105-375. A unit also may employ the remedies of levy and attachment and garnishment against personal property to enforce the collection of delinquent fees. G.S. 105-366; G.S. 105-367; G.S. 105-368.

Availability fees and penalties for solid waste disposal facility services. In addition to assessing a fee for actual use of a disposal facility, a city or county may impose a fee for the availability of disposal facilities provided by the local government on all "improved property" that benefits from the

---

3. Note that many local governments, particularly those that do not provide water and wastewater services, include fees for stormwater management services on the property tax bill. This practice is not prohibited by state law, but, unlike solid waste fees, the stormwater management services fees are not a lien on the property served.

4. In the event that the fees are billed subsequent to the year for which they are assessed, the lien attaches January 1 of the calendar year in which the bill is issued.

availability of the facilities. G.S. 160A-314.1(a); G.S. 153A-292(b). The statutes do not define *improved property*, but it likely requires that there be a residential, commercial, or industrial structure on the real property. The owner of the property is assessed the availability fee and is liable for payment, regardless of who occupies the property or premises.

A local government may not "impose an availability fee on property whose solid waste is collected by a county, a city, or a private contractor for a fee if the fee imposed by a county, a city, or a private contractor for the collection of solid waste includes a charge for the availability and use of a disposal facility provided by the county." G.S. 160A-314.1; G.S. 153A-292. Additionally, "[p]roperty served by a private contractor who disposes of solid waste collected from the property in a disposal facility provided by a private contractor that provides the same services as those provided by the city disposal facility is not considered to benefit from a disposal facility" provided by the local government and is not subject to the availability fee. G.S. 160A-314.1(a); G.S. 153A-292(b). If the services provided at the private contractor's disposal facility are not coextensive with those provided by the local government, the unit may assess an availability fee to cover the costs of the additional services. For example, if a private hauler's disposal facility does not provide recycling services but the local government's disposal facilities do, the local government may impose an availability fee on residents served by the private hauler to cover the costs of the recycling services.

Availability fees for solid waste disposal facility services may be billed along with the fees for other enterprise services provided by the local government, G.S. 160A-314(b); G.S. 153A-277(b), or on the property tax bill. G.S. 160A-314.1(b); G.S. 153A-293. If the fees are included on the property tax bill and designated by ordinance as collectible in the same manner as property taxes, the fees are a lien on the underlying real property described in the property tax bill.

38. Is the owner of a property or premises liable for a fee assessed for the availability of *water* and *wastewater* services if the property, or premises located on the property, is connected to the local government's utility lines but the property or premises is not occupied?

Likely no. A city or county is authorized to require an owner of developed property that contains one or more residential dwelling units or a commercial establishment and is located within a reasonable distance of any water line or wastewater collection line owned, leased, or operated by the city or on behalf of the city to connect the owner's premises with the water or wastewater line or both.[5] In lieu of requiring the property owner to connect to the water or wastewater lines, the local government may require the payment of a periodic availability charge, as long as the fee does not exceed the minimum periodic service or administrative charge assessed to properties that are connected. G.S. 153A-284; G.S. 160A-317. Based on the express language of the statute, however, there likely is no authority to assess an availability fee if the property or premises is actually connected to the unit's water or wastewater lines. That is, there likely is no authority to assess an availability fee on a dry tap.

Once a property or premises is connected to the local government's water or wastewater utility systems, however, the local government may assess a periodic administrative fee that applies even at a zero consumption level.

39. Is the owner of a property or premises liable for a fee assessed for the availability of *solid waste disposal* services if the property, or premises located on the property, is not occupied?

Likely yes, if the property is improved. A city or county is authorized to assess three different fees for solid waste services: (1) a fee for the collection of solid waste by the local government, (2) a fee for the use of a disposal facility provided by the local government, and (3) an availability fee for the availability of disposal facilities provided by the local government. G.S. 153A-292; G.S. 160A-314, -314.1, and -317.

---

5. A local government does not have the authority to require property in industrial use to connect to its water or wastewater systems.

Subject to a few exceptions, the fee for the availability of disposal facilities may be assessed on all "improved property" in a city or county that benefits from the availability of the solid waste facilities, regardless of whether or not the property is occupied or the services are actually used.[6] The statutes do not define *improved property*, but it likely requires that there be a residential, commercial, or industrial structure on the real property. A city or county may not "impose an availability fee on property whose solid waste is collected by a county, a city, or a private contractor for a fee if the fee imposed by a county, a city, or a private contractor for the collection of solid waste includes a charge for the availability and use of a disposal facility provided by the county." G.S. 160-314.1(a); G.S. 153A-292(b). Additionally, "[p]roperty served by a private contractor who disposes of solid waste collected from the property in a disposal facility provided by a private contractor that provides the same services as those provided by the [local government's] disposal facility is not considered to benefit from a disposal facility" provided by the local government and is not subject to the availability fee. G.S. 160A-314.1(a); G.S. 153A-292(b). If the services provided at the private contractor's disposal facility are not coextensive with those provided by the local government, the unit may assess an availability fee to cover the costs of the additional services. For example, if a private hauler's disposal facility does not provide recycling services but the local government's disposal facilities do, the local government may impose an availability fee on residents served by the private hauler to cover the costs of the recycling services.

6. Note that the statutes state, in relevant part, that "[a] fee for availability . . . may be imposed on all improved property in the [city or county] that benefits from the availability of the facility." G.S. 160A-314.1; G.S. 145A-292(b). The statutes define two situations in which improved property is not deemed to "benefit" from the availability of a disposal facility. Arguably, the two exceptions are not exclusive and a local government may not assess an availability fee on any improved property that does not benefit from the availability of a disposal facility provided by the unit even if the property does not qualify for one of the specifically defined exceptions. Under this interpretation, local governments have broad discretion in determining what improved property benefits from the availability of a disposal facility. Several local governments have adopted an approach whereby the availability fee is assessed on all improved property unless the property owner demonstrates that the property is not receiving electric service or unless a certificate of occupancy has not been issued.

40. Is the owner of a property or premises liable for a fee assessed for the availability of *solid waste collection* services if the property, or premises located on the property, is not occupied?

No. A local government may not impose a solid waste collection fee on any property that does not receive collection services provided by the local government. A city (but not a county), however, may require any owner of "improved property" to participate in solid waste collection services provided by the city if the owner or occupant of the property has not otherwise contracted for the collection of solid waste from the property. G.S. 160A-317(b). The statute does not define *improved property*, but it likely requires that there be a residential, commercial, or industrial structure on the real property. A city may assess a fee for the collection services, as long as the fee does not exceed the costs of collection.

41. If a tenant establishes a public enterprise utility account with a local government and fails to pay for the water, wastewater, or solid waste services provided, may the owner of the property or premises be held liable for the unpaid fees?

Generally no. In most cases, only the contracting party is liable for public enterprise utility fee payments. G.S. 153A-277(c); G.S. 160A-314(c). Thus the liability for public enterprise utility fees may not be transferred from a tenant-customer to the owner of the property or premises served.

There are two exceptions to the general rule that only the contracting party is liable for utility fees. The owner of the property is legally obligated to pay the public enterprise utility services fees for any public enterprise services, even if the owner is not the contracting party, if (1) the property served is leased or rented to more than one tenant and services rendered to more than one tenant are measured by the same meter, or (2) the fees for the use of a sewage system are billed separately from the fees for the use of a water distribution system. G.S. 153A-277(d); G.S. 160A-314(d). The fees are not a lien on the real property or premises served, though. G.S. 153A-277(c); G.S. 160A-314(c).

In addition to the two exceptions, a local government is authorized to adopt an ordinance providing that any fees for collecting or disposing of solid waste, or for the availability of solid waste disposal facilities, may be billed with the property taxes and payable in the same manner as property taxes. If a local government includes the fees for solid waste services on the property tax bill, any delinquent fees may be collected in the same manner by which delinquent personal or real property taxes are collected. G.S. 160A-314.1(b); G.S. 153A-293. The fees are the liability of the owner of the property or premises served, regardless of who occupies the property or premises. Moreover, the fees are a lien on the real property described on the bill that includes the fees.

Finally, a local government may require another party to enter into a contractual agreement to pay any fees owed in the event of a default by the primary account holder. For example, a local unit may require the owner of rental property to co-sign the application for the public enterprise utility service, thereby agreeing to be liable for any delinquent fees owed by a tenant. Absent such a written contractual agreement, however, a local government may not transfer legal liability for the fees to another party.

42. May a local government recover payment for public enterprise utility services provided to an individual or nongovernment entity if it does not have a contract with the individual or nongovernment entity to which it is providing services?

Likely yes. Under certain circumstances a local government may be able to enforce liability for utility fees in the absence of a contractual agreement based on a theory of quasi contract, or contract implied-in-law. A contract implied-in-law is not a contract and is not based on an actual agreement. It is a theory of recovery for the reasonable value of services rendered to prevent unjust enrichment. North Carolina courts generally have allowed recovery based on quasi contract if the following requirements are satisfied: "(1) services were rendered to the defendants; (2) the services were knowingly and voluntarily accepted; and (3) the services were not given gratuitously."[7] For example, in *Orange Water & Sewer Authority v. Town of Carrboro*,[8] the North Carolina Court of Appeals held that the town was liable to the water and sewer authority for fire hydrant rental charges even though there was no explicit contract. Noting that "[a]n implied contract rests on the equitable principle that one

---

7. Envtl. Landscape Design Specialist v. Shields, 75 N.C. App. 304, 330 S.E.2d 627 (1985).

8. 58 N.C. App. 676, 294 S.E.2d 757 (1982).

should not be allowed to enrich himself unjustly at the expense of the other and on the principle that what one ought to do, the law supposes him to have promised to do," the court found sufficient evidence of an implied agreement between the water and sewer authority and the town requiring the town to make reasonable rental payments for the hydrants.[9]

Note: The validity of cases, such as Orange Water & Sewer Authority, *that allow recovery against a government entity under a quasi-contract theory is called into question in light of more recent decisions purporting to extend sovereign immunity protections to counties and municipal corporations.[10] These cases do not prohibit a local government from seeking recovery under a quasi-contract theory against a nongovernment entity, however.*

Moreover, courts in several other jurisdictions have allowed local governments to recover for moneys owed by nongovernment customers for utility services rendered absent a contractual agreement.[11]

If a local government seeks recovery for public enterprise utility services provided in the absence of a contractual agreement, the recovery likely is limited to the minimum service or administrative fees and reasonably calculable usage fees in effect during the period at issue. A unit is further limited in its recovery by the statutory limitations period for collecting outstanding fees.

---

9. Note that the provision of water services constitutes a sale of goods under Article 2 of the Uniform Commercial Code. G.S. 25-2-201 provides that contracts for the sale of goods for $500 or more are not enforceable unless the agreement is evidenced by a writing. Absent a writing, however, a contract for the sale of goods may be enforced if the goods have been received and accepted. G.S. 25-2-201(3)(c). Also, with respect to cities only, G.S. 160A-16 requires that all contracts made by or on behalf of a city be in writing. If a contract is not in writing, it is "void and unenforceable." A city's governing board, however, may expressly ratify an action after the fact to avoid this result. G.S. 160A-16.

10. *See* Whitfield v. Gilchrist, 348 N.C. 39, 497 S.E.2d 412 (1998); Data General Corp. v. County of Durham, 143 N.C. App. 97, 545 S.E.2d 243 (2001).

11. *See, e.g.,* Po River Water & Sewer Co. v. Indian Acres Club of Thornburg, Inc., 495 S.E.2d 478 (Va. 1998) (holding that a promise to pay was implied from the defendant's acceptance and receipt of utility services). Note that some courts also have allowed recovery on a theory of contract implied-in-fact, where the "meeting of the minds is shown by the surrounding circumstances which made it inferable that the contract exists as a matter of tacit understanding." Dayton Power & Light Co. v. KMG Investors I, LP, 1994 WL 29865, at *1 (Ohio Ct. App. Jan. 12, 1994).

The limitations period for a contract implied-in-law is three years.[12] A cause of action on a contract implied-in-law theory likely accrues, triggering the beginning of the limitations period, at the end of each billing cycle in which the entity receiving services should have been billed.[13]

43. May a local government recover payment for public enterprise utility services provided to a local government (that is, a county or municipality) if it does not have a contract with the government entity to which it is providing services?

Likely no. In *Orange Water & Sewer Authority v. Town of Carrboro*,[14] the North Carolina Court of Appeals allowed recovery against a town for services provided by a water and sewer authority even though there was no explicit contract authorizing the services.[15] A more recent case by the court of appeals, however, holds that a local government may not be sued for recovery in the absence of an explicit contractual agreement.[16] According to the court, the doctrine of sovereign immunity "renders this state, including counties and municipal corporations herein, immune from suit absent express consent to be sued or waiver of the right of sovereign immunity."[17] Sovereign immunity

12. *See* Ingram v. Smith, 16 N.C. App. 147, 191 S.E.2d 390 (1972) (holding that contract implied-in-law, or quasi-contract theory, is subject to a three-year limitations period).

13. *See* P-K Tool & Mfg. Co. v. Gen. Elec. Co., 612 F. Supp. 276 (D.C. Ill. 1985). Note that, under certain circumstances, an action to recover payment for public enterprise utility services provided without a contract may constitute an action "for relief on the ground of fraud or mistake." G.S. 1-52(9). If the action is categorized as such, it is still subject to the three-year statutory period, but the period does not begin to run until the fraud or mistake is discovered or should have been discovered through reasonable efforts.

14. 58 N.C. App. 676, 294 S.E.2d 757 (1982).

15. See Question 42.

16. Data General Corp. v. County of Durham, 143 N.C. App. 97, 545 S.E.2d 243 (2001); *see also* Whitfield v. Gilchrist, 348 N.C. 39, 497 S.E.2d 412 (1998).

17. *Id.* at 100, 545 S.E.2d at 246. Arguably, the Data General decision mischaracterizes the protection afforded to local governments; local units likely are insulated from a suit based on quasi-contract because of governmental immunity protection, not sovereign immunity protection. As stated by the North Carolina Supreme Court in *Evans v. Housing Authority of the City of Raleigh*, 359 N.C. 50, 602 S.E.2d 668 (2004), "'[u]nder the doctrine of sovereign immunity, the State is immune from suit absent waiver of immunity. Under the doctrine of governmental immunity, a county [or municipality] is immune from suit for the negligence of its employees in the exercise of governmental

may be waived by statute. It also is implicitly waived when a government entity enters into a valid contract. It is not waived, however, if there is no explicit contractual agreement.[18]

44. May a local government recover payment for public enterprise utility services provided to a government entity (that is, a state or federal entity) if it does not have a contract with the government entity to which it is providing services?

No. Although a local government likely may recover payment for the provision of public enterprise utility services without a contract from an individual or nongovernment entity, it may not recover from the state or a state agency, absent a contractual agreement. In *Whitfield, P.A. v. Gilchrist*,[19] the North Carolina Supreme Court held that sovereign immunity bars recovery in an action against the state on a theory of quasi contract or contract implied-in-law. According to the court, "[o]nly when the State has implicitly waived sovereign immunity by expressly entering into a valid contract through an agent of the

---

functions absent waiver of immunity.' These immunities do not apply uniformly. The State's sovereign immunity applies to both its governmental and proprietary functions, while the more limited governmental immunity covers only the acts of a municipality or a municipal corporation committed pursuant to its governmental functions." *Id.* at 53, 602 S.E.2d at 670 (internal citations omitted); *see also* W. Page Keeton et al., Prosser and Keeton on the Law of Torts § 131, at 1051 (5th ed. 1984 & Supp. 1988) ("The traditional rule was that [local governments] held a governmental immunity in tort, but one different both in origin and scope from the 'sovereign' or governmental immunity of the state. Since [local governments] exhibited a corporate or proprietary face as well as a governmental face, the traditional immunity was narrower than the full range of [local government] activities, protecting only the governmental activities and not the proprietary ones."). The distinction between sovereign and governmental immunity has important implications for a local government acting in a proprietary capacity. For example, despite the language in *Data General*, a county or municipality likely could be held liable on a quasi-contract or contract implied-in-law theory if it received services from another entity absent an explicit contractual agreement in its capacity as owner or operator of a public enterprise utility. The distinction likely is not relevant in the situation presented by the question above, however, because when a local government receives public enterprise utility services, such as water, wastewater, or solid waste services, it is not acting in a proprietary capacity; it thus would be immune from suit under the governmental immunity doctrine.

18. *Data General*, 143 N.C. App. at 100, 545 S.E.2d at 246.
19. 348 N.C. 39, 497 S.E.2d 412 (1998).

State expressly authorized by law to enter into such contract may a plaintiff proceed with a claim against the State upon the State's breach."[20]

Courts have allowed quasi-contractual claims against the federal government or a federal agency only where Congress has waived sovereign immunity by statute.[21]

45. May a local government collect the full amount from a customer if it discovers that it underbilled for the public enterprise utility services provided?

Yes. In *City of Wilson v. Carolina Builders of Wilson, Inc.*,[22] the North Carolina Court of Appeals held that even if a local government inadvertently or negligently fails to properly bill for the services, it may collect the full amount for the services it provided.[23] In that case, the city had adopted an ordinance authorizing it to collect any deficiencies in utility payments due to underbillings for a maximum period of twelve months. Subsequently, the city billed one of its electricity customers at one-half the appropriate rate. Upon discovering the error, the city forwarded a corrected bill to the customer that the customer refused to pay. The city sued the customer to recover the unpaid charges and the customer counterclaimed, alleging that the city should be prevented from collecting the fees owed because it negligently failed to properly bill for them. The district court granted summary judgment for the customer on its counterclaim, but the court of appeals reversed, holding that because government-owned utilities may not discriminate in the distribution of enterprise services or the setting of rates, they may not be prevented from collecting the correct amount for the services provided even if they inadvertently or negligently fail to properly bill for the services.

---

20. *Id.* at 43, 497 S.E.2d at 415. *See generally* City of Gainesville v. State of Florida Dep't of Transportation, 920 So. 2d 53 (Fla. Dist. Ct. App. 2005) (holding that waiver of sovereign immunity will not be implied; thus, in order to sue to collect a utility fee, the local government must have a written contract with the state agency).

21. *See* Niagara Mohawk Power Corp. v. Bankers Trust Co. of Albany, N.A, 791 F.2d 242 (2d Cir. 1986).

22. 94 N.C. App. 117, 379 S.E.2d 712 (1989).

23. *Id.* at 121, 379 S.E.2d at 715 (noting that "a majority of jurisdictions which have considered the issue of underbilling by utilities have held that to disallow recovery for underbilling would amount to discriminatory charges").

In fact, a local government likely has an obligation, rooted in general utility law, to collect any moneys owed. Several courts have held that "the statutory policy against rate discrimination not only permits but requires a utility to collect undercharges."[24]

24. Hous. Auth. of the County of King v. Northeast Lake Washington Sewer & Water Dist., 784 P.2d 1284, 1287 (Wash. Ct. App. 1990) (holding that statutory provision requiring water and sewer district to impose uniform charges for the same class of customer or service embodied a policy against rate discriminations and preferences and "bars application of equitable defenses in a utility's claim for inadvertent or negligent undercharges"); Sigal v. City of Detroit, 362 N.W.2d 886 (Mich. Ct. App. 1985) (same); *see also* Roger D. Colton, Protecting Against the Harms of the Mistaken Utility Undercharge, 39 Wash. U. J. Urb. & Contemp. L. 99 (1991) (noting that public utilities assume a statutory and common law duty to provide service at rates that are not discriminatory, which prohibits a utility from providing service at a rate less than its published rates); *cf.* Holloway v. Alabama Power Co., 568 So. 2d 1245 (Ala. Civ. App. 1990) (holding that a customer of a public utility has no defense—either of estoppel or accord and satisfaction—to charges for services that were actually furnished but which had previously been negligently underbilled); Consol. Edison Co. of N.Y. Inc. v. Jet Asphalt Corp., 522 N.Y.S.2d 124 (N.Y. App. Div. 1987) (same); Corp. de Gestion Ste-Foy, Inc. v. Florida Power & Light Co., 385 So. 2d 124 (Fla. Dist. Ct. App. 1980) (same); Chesapeake and Potomac Tel. Co. of Va. v. Bles, 243 S.E.2d 473 (Va. 1978) ("[I]t is apparent that to permit an undercharge, whether intentionally or inadvertently made, is to grant a [prohibited] preferential rebate to a customer. . . ."); Wisconsin Power & Light Co. v. Berlin Tanning & Mfg. Co., 83 N.W.2d 147 (Wis. 1957) (same). *But see* Brown v. Walton Elec. Membership Corp., 531 S.E.2d 712 (Ga. 2000) (rejecting rationale that it is a contravention of public policy to estop the utility from collecting the full amount due for utilities consumed where the customer has been negligently underbilled and holding that customer can assert accord and satisfaction, equitable estoppel, or statute of limitation defenses when a utility sues to recover the correct billing amount); West Penn Power Co. v. Piatt, 592 A.2d 1306 (Pa. Super. Ct. 1991) (holding that a utility customer can raise a defense of detrimental reliance when the customer is mistakenly undercharged by the utility). Although North Carolina courts have not addressed this issue directly, the court in *Carolina Builders* cited a North Carolina Supreme Court decision, *Atlantic Coast Line Railroad v. West Paving Co.*, 228 N.C. 94, 44 S.E.2d 523 (1947), in which the court stated

> [u]nder well settled principles of law and in accord with the statutes enacted to prevent . . . discrimination among shippers, and to provide equal and impartial service to all alike, it was the duty of the plaintiff as a common carrier of freight to collect the full amount at the correct rate for transportation, and where a lawful charge therefore was negligently omitted, or rate misquoted, charge therefore was negligently omitted, or rate misquoted, resulting in undercharge, the carrier was equally bound to exhaust all legal remedies to require payment in full of the proper charge.

Id. at 97, 44 S.E.2d at 525.

Courts in other jurisdictions have considered whether a consumer of a public utility's service may assert the defense of equitable estoppel to preclude the utility from collecting the full amount due when the consumer has been underbilled. (Under the doctrine of equitable estoppel, an individual or entity is held to a representation made or a position assumed where, otherwise, inequitable consequences would result to another who has, in good faith, relied on the representation or position.) The majority of courts have concluded that the public policy of maintaining equality among consumers does not permit the inequality of rates to arise indirectly through the application of estoppel. Thus, where a statute requires a public utility to charge similarly situated customers according to the same rate schedule, "it contravenes public policy to preclude a public utility from collecting the full amount due for its services, even where the public utility has negligently underbilled its customer."[25] Courts similarly have rejected defenses based on the legal doctrine of accord and satisfaction. A successful claim of accord and satisfaction requires that (1) there is a bona fide dispute between two or more parties, (2) there is an agreement to settle that dispute, and (3) there is performance of the agreement. When a utility inadvertently or negligently underbills a customer and later seeks to collect undercharges, there is no accord and satisfaction because there was no dispute at the time the bills were rendered and paid.[26]

A local government likely is subject to a three-year statute of limitations for collecting underpaid wastewater[27] and solid waste utility charges[28] that are billed along with other public enterprise service fees, and a four-year statutory

---

25. Cincinnati Gas & Elec. Co. v. Joseph Chevrolet Co., 791 N.E.2d 1016, 1022 (Ohio Ct. App. 2003); *see also* Boone County Sand & Gravel Co., Inc. v. Owen County Rural Elec. Coop. Corp., 779 S.W.2d 224 (Ky. Ct. App. 1989) (holding also that a customer cannot assert a counterclaim for damages resulting from negligent underbilling in an action by a utility to recover the amount underbilled). Some courts in other jurisdictions have distinguished between mistakes of fact and mistakes of law for purposes of applying the doctrine of equitable estoppel. For example, if there is a mistake in the rate charged, the customer is presumed to have knowledge of the rate. Thus a utility can collect the full amount owed even if it underbilled the customer. On the other hand, if the billing error involved a misread meter or defective meter, which was uniquely within the province of the utility to reasonably discover or prevent, a court might allow a claim of equitable estoppel. *See* Illinois Power Co. v. Champaign Asphalt Co., 310 N.E.2d 463 (Ill. Ct. App. 1974).

26. *See, e.g.*, Consolidated Edison Co. of N.Y. Inc. v. Jet Asphalt Corp., 522 N.Y.S.2d 124 (N.Y. App. Div. 1987).

27. See Question 69.

28. See Question 70.

period for collecting underpaid water utility fees,[29] although it may set shorter limitations periods by ordinance.[30] The statute of limitations period begins to run at the time of the breach of contract; and the breach likely occurs at the end of each billing cycle in which the customer was underbilled.[31] If solid waste utility fees are billed along with property taxes, the unit may recover for an underbilling as an immaterial irregularity under G.S. 105-394 if it resulted from a clerical or administrative error.[32] The statute of limitations likely is ten years from the date the fees became due.[33]

29. See Question 68.

30. In *Wilson v. Carolina Builders of Wilson, Inc.,* 94 N.C. App. 117, 379 S.E.2d 712 (1989), the North Carolina Court of Appeals held that an ordinance allowing the City of Wilson to collect any deficiencies in utility payments due to underbillings for a maximum period of twelve months was valid on its face.

31. A few courts in other jurisdictions have held that the breach occurs and the statutory period begins at the time the utility presents an adjusted bill to reflect the true costs of service and actual amount owed and the customer refuses to pay. Their rationale is that the statutory period does not begin to run when the underbilling occurred because billing errors by a utility are foreseeable and adjusted billing is a foreseeable method of correcting the errors. *See* City of Akron v. Rogers Industrial Products, Inc., 1997 WL 665719, at *3 (Ohio Ct. App. Oct. 8, 1997); *cf.* Holloway v. Alabama Power Co., 568 So. 2d 1245 (Ala. Civ. App. 1990) (holding that three-year statute of limitations on open accounts serves as a bar to bringing the action, not as a limitation on the amount of recovery once the action has been properly filed). Other courts have rejected this rationale, stating that "[u]nder such a rule, there would be no limit to how long parties could extend the limitations period for an unbilled debt." City of Snohomish v. Seattle-Snohomish Mill Co., Inc., 2003 WL 22073066 (Wash. Ct. App. Sept. 8, 2003); *see, e.g.,* City of Colorado Springs v. Timberlane Assocs., 807 P.2d 1177 (Colo. Ct. App. 1991), *aff'd,* 824 P.2d 776 (Colo. 1992) (holding that general statute of limitations applicable to "actions of debt founded upon any contract or liability in action" ran against city as provider of gas service and prohibited city from collecting unpaid utility charges arising from continuing error in billing procedure dating farther back than six years from when suit filed). Instead, a utility's cause of action for undercharges accrues when it has a right to collect the undercharges. Because North Carolina courts have not addressed this issue, the safest assumption for a North Carolina local government is that the right to collect the undercharges arises at the end of each billing cycle in which the customer was underbilled.

32. *See In re* Morgan, ___ N.C. App. ___, 652 S.E. 2d 655 (2007); Catawba County Tax Collector Against Nuzum-Cross Chevrolet, Inc., 59 N.C. App. 332, 296 S.E.2d 499 (1982). G.S. 105-394 states that "[i]mmaterial irregularities in the listing, appraisal, or assessment of property for taxation or in the levy or collection of the property tax . . . shall not invalidate the tax . . . or any process of . . . collection . . . ."

33. See Question 70.

46. May a local government recover payment for public enterprise utility services provided to a customer if the unit failed to send a timely bill for the fees owed?

Likely yes. In *City of Wilson v. Carolina Builders of Wilson, Inc.*,[34] the North Carolina Court of Appeals held that a municipal electric supplier could collect the correct amount for the services it provided even if it inadvertently or negligently failed to bill for the services. Although the court in that case was addressing a slightly different issue—namely, what happens when the bill for public enterprise utility services does not reflect the full amount owed for the services actually provided—the case may be read to stand for the broader principal that a local government may collect all amounts owed, even if it fails to send a bill.[35] To ensure this result, a local government may wish to include language in its initial contract for service stating that the customer is responsible for payment regardless of whether the customer receives a bill.

A local government likely is subject to a three-year statute of limitations for collecting wastewater[36] and solid waste[37] utility charges that are billed along with other public enterprise service fees and a four-year statutory period for collecting water utility fees,[38] although it may set shorter limitations periods by ordinance.[39] The statute of limitations period begins to run at the time of the breach of contract; and the breach likely occurs at the end of each billing cycle in which the customer was provided service.[40] If solid waste utility fees

34. 94 N.C. App. 117, 379 S.E.2d 712 (1989).

35. See Question 45.

36. See Question 69.

37. See Question 70.

38. See Question 68.

39. In *Wilson v. Carolina Builders of Wilson, Inc.*, 94 N.C. App. 117, 379 S.E.2d 712 (1989), the North Carolina Court of Appeals held that an ordinance allowing the City of Wilson to collect any deficiencies in utility payments due to underbillings for a maximum period of twelve months was valid on its face.

40. A few courts in other jurisdictions have held that the breach occurs and the statutory period begins at the time the utility presents an adjusted bill to reflect the true costs of service and the actual amount owed and the customer refuses to pay. Their rationale is that the statutory period does not begin to run when the underbilling occurred because billing errors by a utility are foreseeable and adjusted billing is a foreseeable method of correcting the errors. *See* City of Akron v. Rogers Industrial Products, Inc., 1997 WL 665719, at *3 (Ohio Ct. App. Oct. 8, 1997); *cf.* Holloway v. Alabama Power Co., 568 So. 2d 1245 (Ala. Civ. App. 1990) (holding that three-year statute of limitations

are billed along with property taxes, the unit may recover any unbilled charges under the immaterial irregularity provisions in G.S. 105-394 if the failure to bill for the fees resulted from a clerical or administrative error.[41] The statute of limitations likely is ten years from the date the fees became due.[42]

Note: Although a local government probably may recover fees for public enterprise services provided if it fails to send a bill, it may not be able to collect any late fee penalties for nonpayment. If the ordinance establishing the late fee penalties or the contract establishing service states that the late fee penalty applies to all amounts billed that are not timely paid, a local government likely may not assess the penalty if it fails to send a bill. On the other hand, if the ordinance or contract states that the late fee penalty applies to all amounts owed during the normal billing period, even if not billed, then the penalty likely may be assessed.[43]

---

on open accounts serves as a bar to bringing the action, not as a limitation on the amount of recovery once the action has been properly filed). Other courts have rejected this rationale, stating that "[u]nder such a rule, there would be no limit to how long parties could extend the limitations period for an unbilled debt." City of Snohomish v. Seattle-Snohomish Mill Co., Inc., 2003 WL 22073066 (Wash. Ct. App. Sept. 8, 2003); *see, e.g.,* City of Colorado Springs v. Timberlane Assocs., 807 P.2d 1177 (Colo. Ct. App. 1991), *aff'd,* 824 P.2d 776 (Colo. 1992) (holding that general statute of limitations applicable to "actions of debt founded upon any contract or liability in action" ran against city, as provider of gas service, and prohibited city from collecting unpaid utility charges arising from continuing error in billing procedure dating farther back than six years from when suit filed). Instead, a utility's cause of action for undercharges accrues when it has a right to collect the undercharges. Because North Carolina courts have not addressed this issue, the safest assumption for a North Carolina local government is that the right to collect the undercharges arises at the end of each billing cycle in which the customer was underbilled.

41. *See In re* Morgan, ___ N.C. App. ___, 652 S.E.2d 655 (2007); Catawba County Tax Collector Against Nuzum-Cross Chevrolet, Inc., 59 N.C. App. 332, 296 S.E.2d 499 (1982). G.S. 105-394 states that "[i]mmaterial irregularities in the listing, appraisal, or assessment of property for taxation or in the levy or collection of the property tax . . . shall not invalidate the tax . . . or any process of . . . collection . . . ."

42. See Question 70.

43. *See* Capital Props. Co. v. Pub. Serv. Comm'n, 457 N.Y.S.2d 635, 91 A.D.2d 726 (Supr. Ct. Appellate Div. 3d Dep't 1982).

47. Does a customer have a remedy against a local government if the unit overbills for public enterprise utility services?

Yes. In providing public enterprise utility services, a local government is acting in a proprietary capacity and is not insulated from suit under governmental or sovereign immunity.[44] A customer may bring an action for breach of contract and may have other remedies under tort law.[45]

The statute of limitations for recovering against a local government for overbilling for water or wastewater utility services is two years.[46] G.S. 1-53(1). The same statute of limitations applies to any suit against the local government arising from the contractual relationship with the public enterprise utility services customer. The statute of limitations for recovering against a local government for overbilling for solid waste services billed along with other public enterprise services fees also is two years. If the fees for solid waste services are included on the property tax bill, however, the statute of limitations for recovering against a local government likely is five years after the fees are due or six months after payment of the fees, whichever is later. G.S. 105-381.

---

44. *See, e.g.,* Town of Spring Hope v. Bissette, 305 N.C. 248, 287 S.E.2d 851 (1982).

45. There is, however, no fundamental right to accurate utility bills entitling a customer to substantive due process protections. *See* Chun v. New York City Dep't of Envtl. Protection, 989 F. Supp. 494 (S.D.N.Y. 1998).

46. *See* Jones v. Town of Angier, ___ N.C. App. ___, 638 S.E.2d 607 (2007).

IV Discontinuing Utility Services

48. Is a local government authorized to discontinue public enterprise utility services if a customer is delinquent on payments owed for the utility services?

Yes. Generally, a local government may discontinue any public enterprise services,[1] including water, wastewater, and solid waste utility services, to a customer whose account remains delinquent for more than ten days.[2] G.S. 160A-314(b); G.S. 153A-277(b). A local government may set a longer period by local ordinance; in fact, it is common to set the period at twenty-five or thirty days. If, however, a customer has filed a petition for bankruptcy and owed delinquent utility fees prior to filing for bankruptcy, a local government is prohibited from disconnecting service for at least twenty days (thirty days for Chapter 11 bankruptcies).[3]

In order to compel full payment of all public enterprise utility services that a local government provides, it is common practice for a local government to adopt an ordinance authorizing the combination of the fees for multiple public enterprise services—such as water, wastewater, solid waste, and stormwater management services—on the same bill and assigning the order of partial payments such that the fees for the most essential service,

---

1. A county is authorized to provide public enterprise services for water, wastewater, solid waste collection and disposal, airports, off-street parking facilities, public transportation systems, and stormwater management programs. G.S. 153A-274. A city is authorized to provide public enterprise services for water, wastewater, electric, natural gas, public transportation, solid waste collection and disposal, cable television, off-street parking, airports, and stormwater management systems. G.S. 160A-311.

2. Water and sewer authorities may not discontinue service until at least thirty days after fees, rates, and charges become delinquent. G.S. 162A-9(c). Also, if a local government bills for solid waste services along with property taxes, the fees are not considered unless they remain unpaid after January 6 following the due date.

3. See Question 59.

usually water service, are paid last. G.S. 160A-314(b); G.S. 153A-277(b). If an outstanding balance remains on the combined bill after the ten-day period, the local government may discontinue the public enterprise service that remains unpaid.

Note: Discontinuing service to a public enterprise utility services customer may have serious consequences to the occupants of the property or premises served, particularly if wastewater service is discontinued by plugging the sewer. It also may subject the local government to civil liability if done improperly or without cause.[4] A local government should be mindful of these consequences when designing and implementing a service discontinuation policy. A unit, for example, may wish to provide one or more discontinuation notices to the owner or occupants of the property or premises, even if such notices are not legally required.[5] A local government also may choose to inform the local health department upon discontinuing water or wastewater services to a property or premises.

49. May a local government discontinue public enterprise utility services to a property or premises occupied by one or more tenants if the owner of the property or premises is the account holder and fails to pay the fees owed for the services provided to the current occupants?

Likely yes. If the owner of the property or premises is the account holder, or otherwise legally liable for the public enterprise utility fees, a local government likely may discontinue public enterprise utility services and refuse to reinstate them until the delinquent amounts are paid in full, even if the property is occupied by one or more tenants.[6] For example, a city or county may discontinue water service to a multi-unit dwelling that is served by a master meter, thereby

---

4. See Question 54.

5. See Question 51.

6. Note that some courts in other jurisdictions have drawn a distinction between delinquent fees for services currently being provided and delinquent fees for services previously provided while another tenant or occupant resided on the property or premises. Under the rationale of these decisions, a local government cannot terminate public enterprise utility services currently being provided at a property or premises for failure of the owner of the property or premises to settle delinquent accounts for services that were previously provided at the property or premises. See Question 10.

shutting off service to all residents of the dwelling, if the owner of the multi-unit dwelling is delinquent on the payments for the water service provided at the premises. The local government likely owes no duty to continue to provide the utility services to occupants of a property or premises unless the occupants are the account holders.

There are two potential claims that a local government does, in fact, owe a duty to a tenant or occupant of a property or premises in addition to the owner: (1) that the tenant is a third-party beneficiary to the contract for utility service between the owner and the local government, or (2) that the tenant has a property interest in continued utility service.

As to the first claim, under North Carolina law, to assert legal rights as a third-party beneficiary to a contractual agreement, the potential third-party beneficiary must establish

> (1) that a contract exists between two persons or entities; (2) that the contract is valid and enforceable; and (3) that the contract was executed for the direct, and not incidental, benefit of the [third party]. A person is a direct beneficiary of the contract if the contracting parties intended to confer a legally enforceable benefit on that person. It is not enough that the contract, in fact, benefits the [third party], if, when the contract was made, the contracting parties did not intend it to benefit the [third party] directly.[7]

Arguably, at least under certain circumstances, a tenant or occupant of a property or premises is the intended direct beneficiary of a contract of public enterprise utility services between the owner of the property or premises and a local government. A tenant or occupant likely would not qualify as a third-party beneficiary, however, unless the contractual language indicates that the parties to the contract intended for the tenant or occupant to have legally enforceable rights.[8]

As to the second claim, to the extent that a tenant or occupant of a property or premises successfully claims a property interest in continued service,[9] such a property interest only triggers certain notice and hearing requirements under the Due Process Clause of the Fourteenth Amendment to the

---

7. Revels v. Miss America Org.,___ N.C. App. ___, 641 S.E.2d 721 (2007).

8. *See* Midkiff v. Adams County Reg'l Water Dist., 409 F.3d 758 (6th Cir. 2005) (rejecting tenant's third-party beneficiary claim).

9. See Questions 51 and 55.

U.S. Constitution; it does not prohibit a local government from terminating the utility services.

A local government must abide by statutory and local ordinance requirements in discontinuing service to a property or premises.[10]

Note: Discontinuing service to a public enterprise utility services customer may have serious consequences on the occupants of the property or premises served, particularly if wastewater service is discontinued by plugging the sewer. It also can subject the local government to civil liability if done improperly or without cause.[11] A local government should be mindful of these consequences when designing and implementing a service discontinuation policy. A unit, for example, may wish to provide one or more discontinuation notices to the owner or occupants of the property or premises, even if such notices are not legally required.[12] A local government also may choose to inform the local health department upon discontinuing water or wastewater services to a property or premises.

50. May a local government discontinue public enterprise utility services to a property or premises that is occupied by one or more tenants at the direction of the owner of the property or premises?

It depends. If the local government has a contract for service with one or more tenants residing at a particular property or premises, the local government does not have the authority to discontinue service at the direction of the owner of the property or premises. The liability of the local government on the contract for service runs to the account holder, not to the owner of the property or premises.

If, however, the owner of the property or premises is the account holder, a local government likely may discontinue service to the owner's property or premises at the owner's direction, even if it is occupied by one or more tenants. The local government likely owes no duty to continue to provide services to occupants of a property or premises unless the occupants are the account holders.[13]

10. See Question 48.
11. See Question 54.
12. See Question 51.
13. See Question 49.

Note: Discontinuing service to a public enterprise utility services customer may have serious consequences to the occupants of the property or premises served, particularly if wastewater service is discontinued by plugging the sewer. It also can subject the local government to civil liability if done improperly or without cause.[14] A local government should be mindful of these consequences when designing and implementing a service discontinuation policy. A unit, for example, may wish to provide one or more discontinuation notices to the owner or occupants of the property or premises, even if such notices are not legally required.[15] A local government also may choose to inform the local health department upon discontinuing water or wastewater services to a property or premises.

51. Is a local government required to provide notice to a delinquent customer before discontinuing public enterprise utility services?

It depends, in part, on the nature of the services, which unit of local government is providing the services, and whether the customer resides within the territorial boundaries of the unit providing the services.

Water and wastewater services. A county is not required to provide notice before disconnecting water and wastewater services to resident customers,[16] G.S. 153A-283, and neither a county nor a city must provide notice before disconnecting water and wastewater services to nonresident customers.[17] G.S. 153A-283; G.S. 160A-312(a). Under existing law, however, it is unclear whether a city must provide notice to its resident customers before discontinuing water and wastewater services.[18]

---

14. See Question 54.

15. See Question 51.

16. *See* McNeill v. Harnett County, 327 N.C. 552, 398 S.E.2d 475 (1990).

17. *See* Southside Trust v. Town of Fuquay-Varina, 69 F. App'x 136 (4th Cir. Jun. 23, 2003); McNeill v. Harnett County, 327 N.C. 552, 398 S.E.2d 475 (1990).

18. The North Carolina Supreme Court has ruled that utility services furnished by a county do not rise to the level of a property interest protected by the North Carolina and United States constitutions because G.S. 153A-283 specifically states that "[i]n no case may a county be held liable for damages for failure to furnish water or sewer services." G.S. 153A-283; *see also* G.S. 162A-87.3 (stating that "in no case shall a county water and sewer district be held liable for damages to those outside the district for failure to furnish services"). With respect to cities, however, the analogous statutory provision states only that "in no case shall a city be held liable for damages to those outside the corporate limits

Solid waste services. A city is not required to provide notice before discontinuing solid waste services to its nonresident customers. G.S. 160A-312(a). As with water and wastewater services, it is unclear whether a city must provide notice to its resident customers before discontinuing solid waste services.

---

for failure to furnish any public enterprise service." G.S. 160A-312(a); *see* Southside Trust v. Town of Fuquay-Varina, 69 F. App'x 136 (4th Cir. Jun. 23, 2003).

The Fifth and Fourteenth Amendments to the United States Constitution, together with the Law of the Land Clause of Article I, Section 19, of the North Carolina Constitution, provide that no person shall be deprived of life, liberty, or property without due process of law. Due process requires that before an individual may be deprived of a constitutionally protected interest, the individual must be afforded notice and an opportunity to be heard. Thus, whether or not a local government is required to give notice and an opportunity to be heard to the contracting party before disconnecting public enterprise utility services depends on whether the customer has a property interest in, or entitlement to, the continued services. Whether a customer has a property interest is determined by state law. In *Memphis Light, Gas & Water Div. v. Craft*, 436 U.S. 1 (1978), the United States Supreme Court held that, under Tennessee law, a local government–owned utility could not terminate services to a customer for failure to pay a disputed utility bill without affording the customer notice and an opportunity to be heard. The Court based its decision on a provision of Tennessee law that obligated utilities to provide service "to all of the inhabitants of the city of its location alike, without discrimination, and without denial, except for good and sufficient cause . . . . and [prohibited the utilities from] terminat[ing] service except for nonpayment of a just service bill." *Id.* at 11 (internal quotations omitted). North Carolina has no statutory provision explicitly prohibiting termination of public enterprise utility services except for just cause. Furthermore, no provision of North Carolina's enterprise statutes requires a local government to provide service to any particular individual or group. Arguably, the lack of any direct statutory provision requiring continued service suggests that North Carolina public enterprise utility customers do not have a property interest in public enterprise services.

On the other hand, the North Carolina public enterprise statutes do provide that services may be terminated after ten days for nonpayment of all fees for public enterprise services that are legally due and owing to the city. G.S. 160A-314(b). Arguably, the provisions are analogous to the provision at issue in *Craft* and do, in fact, create a property interest in continued service as long as all fees actually due and owing are paid. If so, a customer must receive notice and be afforded an opportunity to dispute any fees before services may be disconnected.

Additionally, several North Carolina courts have equated the duty of local government–owned utilities to that of public utilities even though local government–owned utilities are specifically excluded from the definition of "public utility" in G.S. 62-3(23)(d) and are not subject to regulation by the North Carolina Utilities Commission. *See* City of Wilson v. Carolina Builders of Wilson, Inc., 94 N.C. App.

Unlike with water and wastewater services, it also is unclear whether a county can discontinue solid waste services to resident and nonresident customers, although, practically, this issue is unlikely to arise.[19]

Note: Discontinuing service to a public enterprise utility services customer may have serious consequences to the occupants of the property or premises served, particularly if wastewater service is discontinued by plugging the sewer. It also can subject the local government to civil liability if done improperly or without cause.[20] A local government should be mindful of these consequences when designing and implementing a service discontinuation policy. A unit, for example, may wish to provide one or more discontinuation notices to the owner or occupants of the property or premises, even if such notices are not legally required. A local government also may choose to inform the local health department upon discontinuing water or wastewater services to a property or premises.

117, 379 S.E.2d 712 (1989) ("Public utilities, including utilities owned by cities, may not discriminate in the distribution of services or the setting of rates."). In *Dale v. City of Morganton*, 270 N.C. 567, 155 S.E.2d 136 (1967), for example, the North Carolina Supreme Court stated that "the right of a municipal corporation operating a plant for the [provision of utility services] to its inhabitants to refuse to serve is neither greater nor less than that of a privately owned [company] to do so." *Id.* at 572, 155 S.E.2d at 141. And the court noted that "[a] public-service corporation cannot arbitrarily refuse to supply one of a class which it has undertaken to serve. It must justify its refusal by good reasons." *Id.* In *Dale*, the court was dealing with the issue of refusing to serve a customer, not disconnecting service. At least a few local government attorneys, however, have interpreted this language to indicate that utility customers in North Carolina have a property interest in utility service.

Note that even if a city's resident customers have a property interest in continued water or wastewater services, it only triggers certain notice and hearing requirements before services may be discontinued. See Question 52. It does not prohibit discontinuation of services altogether. It also does not suggest that a city may be held liable for failing to furnish a sufficient supply of water to carry out its governmental functions, such as fire protection.

19. Many courts have strained to interpret state statutes as granting a property interest in traditional utility services, such as water, wastewater, and electricity, because such services have "become almost a necessity for safety and comfort in modern-day life." C.E. Tucker v. Hinds County, 558 So. 2d 869, 874 (Miss. 1990). It is less likely that a court would consider solid waste services equally necessary, and thus less likely that it would interpret the statutory language as granting a property interest in solid waste services.

20. See Question 54.

52. If a local government is required to provide notice to a delinquent public enterprise utility services customer before discontinuing service, what information must it provide?

To the extent that a local government is required to provide notice to a delinquent public enterprise utility services customer before discontinuing service,[21] it may provide sufficient notice in a number of ways—including a statement on the monthly bill or on the initial contract establishing utility service. The statement should advise customers that the enterprise service will be terminated "X" number of days after the balance owed becomes due. [The public enterprise statutes mandate that at least ten days be allowed before service is disconnected,[22] but a local government may allow for a longer grace period. G.S. 160A-314(b); G.S. 153A-277(b).] The notice also should inform the customer of a procedure for disputing any public enterprise fees, including, at a minimum, the contact information—a contact name, contact number, and hours during which the contact person is available—for an individual with the authority to resolve disputed accounts.[23]

Note: If a public enterprise utility services fee is disputed, a local government should not discontinue service until the dispute is resolved.[24]

53. Is a local government required to send a second notice before discontinuing public enterprise utility services for failure to pay a delinquent bill?

No. To the extent that notice is required,[25] once a customer receives an initial notice of the circumstances under which service may be discontinued and the procedures for disputing a bill, the local government is not required to send any additional notices or mark the property where services will be discontinued before terminating services according to the terms specified in the initial notice. If a public enterprise utility fee is disputed, however, a local government should not discontinue service until the dispute is resolved.

21. See Question 51.
22. Water and sewer authorities cannot discontinue service until at least thirty days after fees, rates, and charges become delinquent. G.S. 162A-9(c).
23. *See* Memphis Light, Gas & Water Div. v. Craft, 436 U.S. 1 (1978).
24. See Question 54.
25. See Question 51.

Note: Discontinuing service to a public enterprise utility services customer may have serious consequences to the occupants of the property or premises served, particularly if wastewater service is discontinued by plugging the sewer. It also can subject the local government to civil liability if done improperly or without cause.[26] *A local government should be mindful of these consequences when designing and implementing a service discontinuation policy. A unit, for example, may wish to provide one or more discontinuation notices to the owner or occupants of the property or premises, even if such notices are not legally required.*[27] *A local government also may choose to inform the local health department upon discontinuing water or wastewater services to a property or premises.*

54. May a local government discontinue public enterprise utility services for nonpayment of delinquent fees if a customer disputes the amount owed?

Yes, but the local government risks being held liable for wrongful disconnection of service if the fees are not in fact owed. A local government may be sued for breach of contract and other civil law violations if it wrongfully discontinues public enterprise utility services. In providing public enterprise utility services, a local government is acting in a proprietary capacity and is not insulated from suit under governmental or sovereign immunity.[28]

Moreover, to the extent that a local government fails to provide notice and an opportunity to dispute public enterprise utility fees (if required)[29] before discontinuing services, the employees and officials of a local government may be subject to liability, under federal law, for failing to comply with the due process requirements of the Fourteenth Amendment to the U.S. Constitution: 42 U.S.C. § 1983 gives a right of action to any person whose constitutional rights are violated by a person acting under color of state law and authorizes a successful party to recoup attorneys' fees.

---

26. See Question 54.

27. See Question 51.

28. *See, e.g.*, Town of Spring Hope v. Bissette, 305 N.C. 248, 287 S.E.2d 851 (1982). Note, however, that a local government may not be held liable for failing to furnish a sufficient supply of water to carry out its governmental functions, such as fire protection.

29. See Question 51.

55. Is a local government required to provide notice to the occupants of a property or premises before discontinuing service if the owner of the property or premises is delinquent on public enterprise utility fee payments for service provided to the property or premises?

Likely no. To the extent that any notice is required,[30] the local government's obligation likely extends only to the contracting party. Thus, if the owner of the property or premises established the account, the local government is required only to provide notice to the owner before discontinuing services; the local government is not required to provide notice to any tenants or occupants residing on the property or premises.[31]

Note: Discontinuing service to a public enterprise utility services customer may have serious consequences to the occupants of the property or premises served, particularly if wastewater service is discontinued by plugging the sewer. It also can

30. See Question 51.

31. *See* Golden v. City of Columbus, 404 F.3d 950 (6th Cir. 2005) (holding that tenant did not have property interest in a city's provision of water service protected by due process); Midkiff v. Adams County Reg'l Water Dist., 409 F.3d 758 (6th Cir. 2005); Sterling v. Village of Maywood, 579 F.2d 1350 (7th Cir. 1978) (same); *see also* Hayes v. Niagara Mohawk Power Corp., 281 N.E.2d 843 (1972) (holding that utility did not have to give tenant notice of termination because the tenant did not have a contractual relationship with the utility); Marrero v. Garcia Irizarry, 829 F. Supp. 523 (D. Puerto Rico, 1993) (holding that residents who had not entered into a contract with the utility for water services had no constitutionally protected interests). *But see* Davis v. Weir, 328 F. Supp. 317 (N.D. Ga. 1971), *aff'd on other grounds*, 497 F.2d 139 (5th Cir. 1974) (holding that where city had duty to provide water to all residents of municipality on application, city was not entitled to terminate water service to an apartment tenant who was the actual user of the water service without notice to the tenant even though the water service was being terminated because of the landlord's nonpayment of charges). A few courts have recognized a property interest in a tenant's right, under landlord–tenant law, to bring an action to enjoin the tenant's landlord from constructively evicting the tenant by terminating water service or declining to pay for it. The courts reason that depriving a tenant of the right to seek injunctive relief by failing to give proper notice before terminating utility service violates due process. *See* Turpen v. City of Corvallis, 26 F.3d 978 (9th Cir. 1994), *cert. denied*, 513 U.S. 963; DiMassimo v. City of Clearwater, 805 F.2d 1536 (11th Cir. 1986). It is unlikely, though, that North Carolina courts would recognize such a property interest based on North Carolina landlord–tenant law.

subject the local government to civil liability if done improperly or without cause.[32] *A local government should be mindful of these consequences when designing and implementing a service discontinuation policy. A unit, for example, may wish to provide one or more discontinuation notices to the owner or occupants of the property or premises, even if such notices are not legally required.*[33] *A local government also may choose to inform the local health department upon discontinuing water or wastewater services to a property or premises.*

56. May a local government discontinue public enterprise utility services at one property or premises because the contracting party is delinquent on an account for public enterprise utility services provided at another property or premises?

Maybe. Although there is no North Carolina case law on point, several courts that have addressed this issue hold that a utility may not cut off or refuse service to a customer at one property or premises for failure to pay for utility service furnished at a different location and under a separate contract.[34] The reasoning

32. See Question 54.
33. See Question 51.
34. *See, e.g.,* Komisarek v. New England Tel. & Tel. Co., 282 A.2d 671 (N.H. 1971) (holding that if utility company intended to assert the right to terminate any service other than that for which the delinquent payment was due, "it was incumbent upon it to make this plain to its consumers by its tariff"); Benson v. Paris Mountain Water Co., 70 S.E. 897 (S.C. 1910) (holding that a water company had no right to cut off the water from a consumer at one place to which it was supplied under contract for refusal of such consumer to pay a bill for water furnished him at another time and place, under another contract); Gas-Light Co. of Baltimore v. Colliday, 1866 WL 2012 (Md. Ct. App. May 10, 1866) ("[W]here several contracts are made between the same parties for different pieces of property, each requiring its own meter, as in this case, a failure to comply with any terms in relation to one, furnished no excuse or ground to the company to withhold the gas from the other."); *cf.* Miller v. Roswell Gas & Elec. Co., 166 P. 1177 (N.M. 1917) ("The authorities are uniform to the effect that a refusal to furnish water or light cannot be sustained merely because the consumer declines and refused to pay for past-due service for some other and independent use, or at some other place or residence."); Hatch v. Consumers' Co., 104 Pac. 670 (Idaho 1909), *aff'd on other grounds,* 224 U.S. 148 ("A water company cannot enforce a rule requiring a consumer to pay an old or disputed bill for water furnished him at some previous time, or some other and independent use, or at some other place or residence, or for a separate or distinct transaction from that for which he is claiming and demanding a water supply, as a condition precedent to supplying him with

is that a local government is obligated to collect moneys owed in the usual way in which debts are collectible and cannot force payment by discontinuing or refusing service under a new contract.

Not all cases are in accord. A few courts have sustained the right of a utility to discontinue or refuse service because of nonpayment of charges for service at a different property or premises, without regard to any statutory, regulatory, or contract provisions.[35] Other courts have upheld discontinuance of service at an address other than that at which the overdue charges were incurred where the contract employed by the particular utility in its transactions with customers specifically provided that it could deny service for the nonpayment of charges arising "under this contract or any other contract."[36] And at least one court has held that a utility can cut off a customer's service at one address because of his refusal to pay a bill for utility services furnished to him at another time and place and under another contract, as long as it proceeds fairly.[37]

---

water, where he tenders payment of the established water rate in advance for the service he is demanding."); Elwell v. Atlanta Gas Light Co., 181 S.E. 599 (Ga. Ct. App. 1935) (observing that although a utility company has the right to require a reasonable deposit as security for the payment of service to be rendered, it may not refuse service to a consumer merely because he declines or refuses to pay a bill for past service rendered at some other place); Merrill v. Livermore Falls Light & Power Co., 105 A. 120 (Me. 1918) (holding that a utility cannot refuse to supply a consumer merely because he refuses to pay an overdue bill for service at some location other than that for which he is demanding a supply).

35. See Mackin v. Portland Gas Co., 61 P. 134 (Ore. 1900) (holding that gas company's rule that, in the event of a default, the company could continue the supply of gas until payment is made authorized the gas company to discontinue service to a customer "at one set of premises until payment should be made of [the] delinquent bill for gas furnished him at another" premises).

36. See Clark v. Utica Gas & Elec. Co., 224 A.D. 448 (N.Y. App. Div. 1928) (holding that statutory provision providing that any person who should "neglect or refuse to pay the rent or remuneration due for the same" justified an electric company's termination of service to a customer's current residence because of his refusal to pay an overdue bill for electricity supplied at his previous residence). But see Meridian L. & R. Co. v. Steele (83 So. 414 (Miss. 1919) (holding that a provision in a contract specifying that a utility could discontinue service for the nonpayment of charges incurred "upon such premises or elsewhere" was without consideration insofar as it gave the utility the right to refuse service at the location covered thereby until the customer paid an overdue bill for service rendered at an earlier address).

37. Water Supply Bd. of City of Arab v. Williams, 302 So. 2d 534 (Ala. Civ. App. 1974); cf. Josephson v. Mountain Bell, 576 P.2d 850 (Utah 1978) (Hall, J. dissenting) (noting splitting of authority on issue but arguing that a utility has a right to deny service

Note: Discontinuing service to a public enterprise utility services customer may have serious consequences to the occupants of the property or premises served, particularly if wastewater service is discontinued by plugging the sewer. It also can subject the local government to civil liability if done improperly or without cause.[38] *A local government should be mindful of these consequences when designing and implementing a service discontinuation policy. A unit, for example, may wish to provide one or more discontinuation notices to the owner or occupants of the property or premises, even if such notices are not legally required.*[39] *A local government also may choose to inform the local health department upon discontinuing water or wastewater services to a property or premises.*

57. Is a local government authorized to discontinue one public enterprise utility service if a customer fails to pay for another public enterprise utility service?

No. But a local government may include fees for any of the enterprise services provided by a local government on the same bill.[40] G.S. 160A-314(b) and G.S. 153A-277(b). And a unit's governing board may adopt an ordinance specifying the order of partial payments for any of the fees billed on the same bill. Failure to pay the entire bill may result in discontinuation of the public enterprise services remaining unpaid according to the partial payment allocation.[41]

For example, assume a local government provides water services for a $5.50 monthly charge, wastewater services for $11.00 per month, and solid waste collection and disposal services for $16.00 per month. Assume also that the local government includes all three fees on the same monthly bill and, by ordinance,

---

at one address because of failure to pay for past service rendered at another address if the public utility's "actions are arbitrary, unjust, inequitable, or without legal right under the particular circumstances").

38. See Question 54.

39. See Question 51.

40. The services include electric, water, wastewater, gas, public transportation, solid waste, cable television, off-street parking, airports, and stormwater management for cities, G.S. 160A-311, and water, wastewater, solid waste, airports, off-street parking, public transportation, and stormwater management for counties. G.S. 153A-274.

41. *See generally* Perez v. City of San Bruno, 616 P.2d 1287 (Cal. 1980) (holding that city, which provided water, wastewater, and garbage services to its citizens and which billed for those services by means of a single unified statement, could constitutionally resort to the remedy of cessation of water service when a citizen failed to make full and complete payment for the municipal services rendered).

allocates partial payments to cover the solid waste services fee first, the wastewater service fee second, and the water service fee last. The total amount owed for the month is $32.50. If a customer pays only $28.00, the payment covers the solid waste fee and the wastewater fee, but it does not cover the full water fee. Thus the local government may discontinue water service for nonpayment, in accordance with state law and its local policy. If a customer pays only $18.00, the payment covers the solid waste fee, but it does not cover the full wastewater fee or any of the water fee. In that case, the local government may discontinue both wastewater and water service for nonpayment, in accordance with state law and its local policy.

Note: Discontinuing service to a public enterprise utility services customer may have serious consequences to the occupants of the property or premises served, particularly if wastewater service is discontinued by plugging the sewer. It also can subject the local government to civil liability if done improperly or without cause.[42] A local government should be mindful of these consequences when designing and implementing a service discontinuation policy. A unit, for example, may wish to provide one or more discontinuation notices to the owner or occupants of the property or premises, even if such notices are not legally required.[43] A local government also may choose to inform the local health department upon discontinuing water or wastewater services to a property or premises.

58. May a local government discontinue public enterprise utility services to a property or premises if the owner of the property or premises, or the nonowner account holder, fails to pay the property tax bill or other local taxes and fees unrelated to the public enterprise utility services?

No. When a local government provides utility services, it acts in a proprietary capacity. In *Dale v. City of Morganton*,[44] the North Carolina Court of Appeals held that a local government's right to provide service it renders in its capacity as a utility provider must be determined separately from the functions it performs in its role as a unit of government. A local government must resort to the specific statutory remedies to collect delinquent property taxes and other

---

42. See Question 54.
43. See Question 51.
44. 270 N.C. 567, 155 S.E.2d 136 (1967).

local taxes and fees, even if the other taxes or fees are included on the same bill as the public enterprise utility fees.

59. May a local government discontinue public enterprise utility services to a customer who has filed for bankruptcy if the customer is delinquent on utility fee payments that arose *prior* to the filing of the petition for bankruptcy (that is, pre-petition debts)?

No, at least for a certain period of time. Federal bankruptcy law—specifically 11 U.S.C. § 366(a)—prohibits a utility providing utility services, once a customer has filed a petition for bankruptcy,[45] from "altering, refusing, or discontinuing service to, or discriminating against, a trustee or a debtor solely on the grounds that the debtor had not paid its prepetition debts when due."

The Bankruptcy Code does not define the term *utility services*, but

> the legislative history indicates that this section was intended to cover those utilities that have a special position with respect to the debtor, "such as an electric company, gas supplier, or telephone company that is a monopoly in the area so the debtor cannot easily obtain comparable services from another utility." Such services as water, electricity, gas, and phones are typically regarded as necessary to meet minimum standards of living.[46]

Based on this understanding, water and wastewater services provided by a local government likely constitute utility services for purposes of Section 366(a). It is less clear whether solid waste disposal and collection services also qualify as utility services. It probably will depend on whether the local government is the exclusive provider of solid waste collection and disposal services, such that

45. There are six types of bankruptcy under the United States Bankruptcy Code, located at Title 11 of the United States Code and designated by chapter number: Chapter 7 (governs basic liquidation for individuals and businesses); Chapter 9 (governs municipal bankruptcies); Chapter 11 (governs rehabilitation or reorganization, primarily by business debtors but sometimes by individuals with substantial debts and assets); Chapter 12 (governs rehabilitation for family farmers and fishermen); Chapter 13 (governs rehabilitation with a payment plan for individuals with a regular source of income); and Chapter 15 (governs ancillary and other international cases). The most common types of personal bankruptcy for individuals are Chapter 7 and Chapter 13. Corporations and other business entities often file under Chapter 7 or Chapter 11.

46. *In re* Moorefield, 218 B.R. 795, 796 (Bankr. M.D.N.C. 1997).

an individual or entity is not able to dispose of waste by an alternative means or at an alternative disposal facility. Even then, a court may find that solid waste services, although important, are not as essential as water, wastewater, and electricity services; therefore solid waste services are not included in the definition of utility services for purposes of this statute.[47]

For all bankruptcies other than Chapter 11,[48] the prohibition in Section 366(a) is conditioned on Section 366(b), which requires that the trustee or debtor furnish "adequate assurance of payment"[49] for post-petition service to the utility within twenty days after the filing of the petition. Such adequate assurance may be in the form of a deposit with the utility or it may be given by "other security," either of which may be modified by order of court on request of a party in interest after notice and a hearing. During the twenty-day period, a local government may issue a demand letter for a deposit or other form of security,[50] but it does not have to do so as a precondition to terminating service according to its usual policy if it does not receive some form of adequate assurance by the end of the twenty days.[51] Section 366(b) does not apply to a debtor who files a Chapter 11 petition; instead, Section 366(c) governs.

If the debtor files a petition for bankruptcy under Chapter 11, a utility "may alter, refuse, or discontinue utility service, if during the thirty-day period beginning on the date of the filing of the petition, the utility does not receive from the debtor or the trustee adequate assurance of payment for utility service that is satisfactory to the utility." Unlike Section 366(b), Section 366(c) defines the term *assurance of payment*, as it applies to Chapter 11 debtors, to include a cash deposit, letter of credit, certificate of deposit, surety bond, prepayment of utility consumption, or another form of security that is mutually agreed on

47. Note that even if solid waste services do not constitute utility services for purposes of 11 U.S.C. § 366, a local government is still subject to the automatic stay provisions of 11 U.S.C. § 362 for collecting pre-petition debts.

48. In Chapter 11 bankruptcy, the debtor runs the day-to-day operations of its business while creditors and the debtor work with the Bankruptcy Court in order to negotiate and complete a plan to allow the debtor to continue to operate and pay its debts.

49. *In re* Marion Steel Co., 35 B.R. 188 (Bankr. N.D. Ohio 1983) (providing detailed analysis of the factors considered in determining what constitutes adequate assurance). Note that most courts have held that the determination of what constitutes adequate assurance is within the exclusive province of the bankruptcy courts. *See, e.g., In re* Coury, 22 B.R. 766 (Bankr. W.D. Pa. 1982).

50. *See In re* Robmac, 8 B.R. 1 (Bankr. N.D. Ga. 1979).

51. *See* Lloyd v. Champaign Tel. Co., 52 B.R. 653 (Bankr. S.D. Ohio 1985).

between the utility and the debtor or the trustee. The statute explicitly states that administrative expense priority does not constitute an assurance of payment. Thus utility providers have greater protections with respect to Chapter 11 debtors. No matter what assurance of payment is agreed upon, however, it still may be modified by court order after a hearing.[52]

Thus, even if otherwise authorized under state law and local ordinance, a local government may not discontinue service to a customer for nonpayment of utility fees once it receives notice that the customer has petitioned for bankruptcy. If, however, the local government does not receive adequate assurance of payment within twenty days after the customer files the petition for bankruptcy (or assurance of payment after thirty days for Chapter 11 debtors), the local government may proceed with any remedies authorized under state law and local ordinances.

At least a few courts have held that Section 366 does not apply merely to the discontinuation of services following the debtor's petition for bankruptcy relief. According to these courts, it also places an affirmative duty on utilities to reinstate previously terminated services upon notice that a customer has filed a bankruptcy petition.[53]

---

52. 11 U.S.C. § 366(c)(3)(B) provides that in making a determination as to whether an assurance of payment by a Chapter 11 debtor is adequate, a court is prohibited from considering "(i) the absence of security before the date of the filing of the petition; (ii) the payment by the debtor of charges for utility service in a timely manner before the date of the filing of the petition; or (iii) the availability of an administrative expense priority."

53. *See, e.g., In re* Whittaker, 882 F.2d 791 (3d Cir. 1989); *In re* Good Time Charlie's Ltd., 25 B.R. 226 (Bankr. E.D. Pa. 1982) (noting that the inclusion of the word "refuse" in the statute, along with the terms "alter" and "discontinue," compelled it to conclude that a pre-petition interference with utility service also came within the statute's ambit). *But cf. In re* Robers, 19 B.R. 808 (Bankr. E.D. Pa. 1983) (holding that utility is not compelled under Section 366(b) to reinstate services during the thirty-day period without a security deposit).

60. May a local government discontinue public enterprise utility services to a customer who has filed for bankruptcy if the customer is delinquent on utility fee payments that arose *after* the filing of the petition for bankruptcy (that is, post-petition debts)?

Yes. Federal bankruptcy law—specifically 11 U.S.C. § 366—prohibits a utility providing utility services, once a customer has filed a petition for bankruptcy, from "altering, refusing, or discontinuing service to, or discriminating against, a trustee or a debtor solely on the grounds that the debtor had not paid its prepetition debts when due." This provision applies only to pre-petition utility debts; it does not apply to delinquent utility payments that arise after the filing of the petition for bankruptcy.[54] With respect to post-petition utility delinquencies, unless the local government and debtor-customer agree otherwise, the local government may pursue any remedies for collecting delinquencies authorized by state law and local ordinance, including discontinuance of public enterprise utility services.

---

54. According to the court in *Jones v. Boston Gas Co.*, ___ B.R. ___, 2007 WL 1651845 (B.A.P. 1st Cir. 2007),

> The purpose of § 366 is "to prevent the threat of termination from being used to collect pre-petition debts while not forcing the utility to provide services for which it may never be paid." Congress sought to strike a balance, in enacting § 366, between the general right of a creditor to refuse to do business with a debtor post-petition, and the debtor's need for utility service.... § 366(b) has been read as an exception to the automatic stay, allowing a utility to alter, refuse or discontinue service for failure to provide adequate assurance of payment without recourse to the bankruptcy court.... Thus, based on a debtor's failure to provide adequate assurance of payment, bankruptcy courts have concluded that § 366(b) grants utilities the unilateral right to terminate service. Courts have logically segued to the conclusion that if failure to provide adequate assurance of payment is grounds for a utility to terminate service, then failure to make post-petition payments likewise allows for termination without requesting permission from the bankruptcy court.... Hence, courts have routinely allowed utilities to terminate service for post-petition delinquencies without obtaining relief from stay.

Id. at *2–3; *see also In re* Webb, 38 B.R. 541, 544 (Bankr. E.D. Pa. 1984) ("In essence, a utility has the discretion to refuse service to any debtor for any reason which would validly constitute a ground for refusal if that debtor were not in bankruptcy, with the single exception of nonpayment for past services.").

Note: Discontinuing service to a public enterprise utility services customer may have serious consequences to the occupants of the property or premises served, particularly if wastewater service is discontinued by plugging the sewer. It also can subject the local government to civil liability if done improperly or without cause.[55] A local government should be mindful of these consequences when designing and implementing a service discontinuation policy. A unit, for example, may wish to provide one or more discontinuation notices to the owner or occupants of the property or premises, even if such notices are not legally required.[56] A local government also may choose to inform the local health department upon discontinuing water or wastewater services to a property or premises.

61. May a local government be held liable for wrongful disconnection of public enterprise utility services?

Yes. A local government may be sued for breach of contract and other civil law violations if it wrongfully disconnects public enterprise utility services. In providing public enterprise utility services, a local government is acting in a proprietary capacity and is not insulated from suit under governmental or sovereign immunity.[57]

Moreover, to the extent that a local government fails to provide notice and an opportunity to dispute public enterprise utility fees (if required)[58] before discontinuing services, the employees and officials of a local government may be subject to liability, under federal law, for failing to comply with the due process requirements of the Fourteenth Amendment to the U.S. Constitution: 42 U.S.C. § 1983 gives a right of action to any person whose constitutional rights are violated by a person acting under color of state law and authorizes a successful party to recoup attorneys' fees.

55. See Question 54.

56. See Question 51.

57. *See, e.g.,* Town of Spring Hope v. Bissette, 305 N.C. 248, 287 S.E.2d 851 (1982). For an explanation of governmental and sovereign immunity protections, see note 17 in Question 43.

58. See Question 51.

62. If a local government discontinues public enterprise utility services because of nonpayment of public enterprise utility service fees, may it be compelled to reconnect or renew service before the fees are paid in full?

Maybe. Generally, a local government may refuse to reconnect or renew public enterprise utility services to a property or premises until it receives payment in full of the utility fees owed.

If, however, the delinquent customer is not the owner of the property or premises served and a new or different tenant or occupant requests utility service, such service must be provided even if the delinquent account is not settled. G.S. 160A-314(b); G.S. 153A-277(b). Moreover, several courts in other jurisdictions have held that even if the customer is the owner of the property or premises served, a local government may not be able to deny service to a tenant, occupant, or new owner before receiving full payment.[59]

63. If a local government provides notice of discontinuation for delinquent public enterprise utility services payments, does it waive its right to discontinue service if it does not do so within the time period specified in the notice?

Maybe. There is no North Carolina case law on point, but a few courts in other jurisdictions have held that a utility that has the right to discontinue service for nonpayment of utility fees but fails to actually cease providing the service within a reasonable time forfeits its right to terminate the service or to refuse to furnish additional service because of such nonpayment.[60] Even if a local government is prohibited from discontinuing service, the unit does not forfeit its right to pursue other authorized collection remedies.

---

59. See Question 11.

60. *See, e.g.,* Hiller v. City of Pinckneyville, 269 Ill. App. 53, 1933 WL 2433 (Ill. App. 4 Dist. 1933) ("If a consumer refuses to pay a bill and the city continues to furnish him water that he pays for, the city will not be permitted to shut off the water because of the nonpayment of the old bill."). Note that in *City of Raleigh v. Fisher,* 232 N.C. 629, 61 S.E.2d 897 (1950), the North Carolina Supreme Court held that a local government could not be estopped from enforcing an ordinance when acting in its governmental capacity. The court's opinion suggests, but does not specifically state, that a local government may waive its right to enforce an ordinance under an estoppel theory while acting in a proprietary capacity. *See also* Holland Group, Inc. v. North Carolina Dep't. of Admin. State Const. Office, 130 N.C. App. 721, 504 S.E. 2d 300 (1998).

64. If a local government discontinues public enterprise utility services because of delinquent payments but does not pursue its legal remedies for collection of the amounts owed within the statutory period allowed, may the unit refuse to reconnect or renew service until the amounts owed are paid in full?

Likely yes, as long as the unit is dealing with the same customer at the same property or premises. If a local government adopts a policy whereby it requires payment in full before renewal of public enterprise utility services, it likely may refuse to provide services to the same customer at the same premises until it receives payment in full, even though the local government could not legally collect the amounts owed in a court of law.[61]

If a different customer is seeking new service at the property or premises, or the same customer is seeking service at a different property or premises, a local government may be prohibited from refusing service.[62]

---

61. *See* Jackson v. Public Serv. Comm'n, 590 A.2d 517 (D.C. Ct. App. 1991) (holding that expiration of statute of limitations did not bar gas company from enforcing terms of its tariff requiring full payment before reinstatement of service). Note that the provisions of G.S. 75-55 likely do not apply to local government–debt collectors. *See* Rea Constr. Co. v. City of Charlotte, 121 N.C. App. 369, 465 S.E.2d 342 (1996).

62. See Questions 11 and 56.

V Other Remedies for Nonpayment

65. Other than discontinuing public enterprise utility services, what methods are available to a local government for collecting delinquent public enterprise utility services fees?

A local government is authorized to collect delinquent public enterprise utility fees "by any remedy provided by law for collecting and enforcing private debts . . . ." G.S. 160A-314(b); G.S. 153A-277(b).

The fees are not a lien on the customer's real or personal property.[1] If, however, a local government obtains a civil judgment against a delinquent customer, it may execute the judgment according to the procedures set forth in G.S. 1, Article 28.

Additionally, if the delinquent fees owed exceed $50, a city or county may take advantage of the state's debt setoff program.[2] G.S. 105A, Art. 1. The debt setoff program allows a local government to submit a delinquent public enterprise utility account to the state to be recouped from any state refund owed to the delinquent customer.[3]

---

1. Note that a few local governments have received authorization through local legislation to treat fees owed for water and wastewater services as if the fees were delinquent property taxes and to collect the amounts due by levying tangible personal property pursuant to G.S. 105-366 and G.S. 105-367. See S.L. 1999-127; S.L. 1998-84; 1989 N.C. Sess. Laws ch. 1070.

2. Note that not all government providers of utility services are entitled to take advantage of the state's debt setoff program. G.S. 105A-2 specifically lists the local agencies entitled to participate: a county; municipality; water and sewer authority (G.S. 162A, Art. 1); regional joint agency created by interlocal agreement (G.S. 160A, Art. 20); public health authority (G.S. 130A, Art. 2, Part 1B); metropolitan sewerage district (G.S. 162A, Art. 5); and a sanitary district (G.S. 130A, Art. 2, Part 2).

3. See Question 66.

Finally, if a local government chooses to include the fees for solid waste services on the property tax bill, it may collect the fees by any remedy authorized for the collection of property taxes.[4]

66. How may a local government take advantage of the state's debt setoff program?

A local government may submit a delinquent public enterprise utility account that is at least $50 to the state to be recouped from a state refund (of at least $50) owed to the delinquent customer. G.S. 105A-4.

Before a local government may submit a debt to the state for collection under the state's debt setoff program, it must provide written notice to the debtor[5] and afford the debtor an opportunity to contest the proposed setoff. The notice must inform the debtor that the local government intends to submit the debt owed for collection by setoff, explain the bases for the unit's claim to the debt, and inform the debtor that the local government intends to apply the debtor's refund against the debt and that a collection assistance fee of $15 will be added to the debt if it is submitted for setoff. The notice also must inform the debtor that the debtor has the right to contest the matter by filing a request for a hearing with the local government and must state the time limits and procedure for requesting the hearing and notify the debtor that failure to request a hearing within the required time will result in setoff of the debt.[6]

---

4. See Question 82.

5. If a local government submits a debt for collection without sending the appropriate notice, it must refund the debtor the entire amount set off plus the collection assistance fee. The portion that reflects the collection assistance fee must be paid from the local government's funds.

6. The following is a sample notice that may be included on all public enterprise utility bills or notices of delinquency:

> As authorized by the North Carolina General Statutes (Chapter 105A, The Setoff Debt Collection Act, as amended; hereinafter cited as the Setoff Act,) the [local government name here] intends to submit the enclosed debt to the North Carolina Department of Revenue (NCDOR). NCDOR will apply the debt against any income tax refund in excess of $50.00 that you may be entitled to receive. Effective January 1, 2003, the Setoff Act authorizes a Local Collection Assistance Fee of $15.00 to be added to your debt submitted and collected through debt setoff. NCDOR is authorized by the Setoff Act to collect this $15.00 collection assistance fee. You have the right to contest this action by filing a written request for a hearing with [local government name here]. You must file your request at the following address no later

A debtor has thirty days after the date the local government mails a notice of a proposed debt setoff to file a written request for a hearing with the governing body of the local government or a person designated by the governing body.[7] The governing body, or a person designated by the governing body, conducts the hearing and determines whether a debt is owed to the local government and in what amount.[8] If the debtor disagrees with the decision, the debtor may file a petition for a contested case within thirty days after the decision, pursuant to G.S. 150B, Article 3.

Once the local government sends the appropriate notice and establishes the debt owed, it must submit the debt to the North Carolina Department of Revenue through one of the following three agencies: the North Carolina League of Municipalities, the North Carolina Association of County Commissioners,[9] or a clearinghouse that has been established pursuant to an interlocal agreement adopted under Article 20 of Chapter 160A of the General Statutes and has agreed to submit debts on behalf of a local government. G.S. 105A-3(b1). A local government should provide the clearinghouse agency with the full name, Social Security number, address, and other pertinent identifying information of the debtor. (A unit should collect this information from a potential public enterprise utility services customer before establishing the account for service.)[10]

---

than thirty days: [contact information here]. Failure to request a hearing within the thirty-day time limit will result in the setoff of the enclosed debt.

7. A request for a hearing is considered to be filed when it is delivered for mailing, properly addressed and with postage prepaid.

8. If a local government submits a debt for collection before final determination of the debt and a decision finds that the local government is not entitled to any part of the amount set off, the local government must send the debtor the entire amount set off plus the collection assistance fee. The portion that reflects the collection assistance fee must be paid from the local government's funds.

9. The N.C. League of Municipalities and the N.C. Association of County Commissioners have created the N.C. Local Government Debt Setoff Clearinghouse to aid local governments in the debt setoff process. For more information, see www.NCsetoff .org (last visited Sept. 1, 2008).

10. A local government may not require that an individual reveal his or her Social Security number as a condition of receiving public enterprise utility services. See Question 2. Furthermore, a local government must inform a potential customer, in writing, (1) that disclosure of the Social Security number is voluntary; (2) under what legal authority the number is solicited; and (3) what uses will be made of the number. Thus, in order to use

67. May a local government use a Social Security number that it collects to establish a new public enterprise utility services account to take advantage of the state's debt setoff program for amounts owed on a separate public enterprise utility services account?

Yes, but only if the customer was clearly informed that the number would be used for this purpose when the number was solicited. G.S. 143-64.60(b); *see also* G.S. 132-1-10(b)(3).

68. What is the statute of limitations period for a local government to sue to collect delinquent *water* utility fees (that is, how long does a local government have to collect)?

The statute of limitations for collecting unpaid water fees likely is four years. G.S. 25-2-725(1). The sale of water by local government utilities constitutes the sale of goods under the Uniform Commercial Code (UCC).[11] Thus it likely is subject to the four-year limitations period set forth in Article 2 of the UCC governing the sale of goods, instead of the general three-year statutory period for actions upon a contract set forth in G.S. 1-52(1).[12] Pursuant to contractual

---

a delinquent customer's Social Security number to aid in debt setoff, a unit must have informed the customer of this potential use prior to obtaining the number.

11. *See* Jones v. Town of Angier, ___ N.C. App. ___, 638 S.E.2d 607 (2007).

12. North Carolina adopted Section 2-725 of the American Law Institute's Model UCC. The Official Comment to the model provision, as well as G.S. 25-2-725, explains that the purpose of the statutory period is "[t]o introduce a uniform statute of limitations for sales contracts, thus eliminating the jurisdictional variations and providing needed relief for concerns doing business on a nationwide scale whose contracts have heretofore been governed by several different periods of limitation depending upon the state in which the transaction occurred. This Article takes sales contracts out of the general laws limiting the time for commencing contractual actions and selects a four year period as the most appropriate to modern business practice." Furthermore, the North Carolina Comment to G.S. 25-2-725 states that Section (1) "changes prior North Carolina Law. Under G.S. 1-52 an action arising out of a simple, nonsealed contract had a statute of limitations of three years from the accrual of the cause of action." [G.S. 1-52(1) provides for a three-year statutory period "[u]pon a contract, obligation or liability arising out of a contract, express or implied . . . ."]

The comments make no mention of G.S. 1-53, which states that a two-year statutory period applies to "[a]n action against a local government upon a contract, obligation or liability arising out of a contract, express or implied." On its face, G.S. 25-2-725 appears to

agreement, however, the parties to the contract for water service can reduce the statutory period to not less than one year. G.S. 25-2-725(1).

The statutory period commences when the cause of action accrues. According to G.S. 25-2-725(2), "[a] cause of action accrues when the breach occurs, regardless of the aggrieved party's lack of knowledge of the breach." A customer's failure to pay water utility fees by the periodic deadline specified by the local government constitutes a breach of the contract.

Note: The statute of limitations may be waived if a customer reaffirms the debt owed.[13] *For example, if a local government offers a payment plan option to delinquent customers and a customer enters into an agreement to repay the fees owed pursuant to the payment plan, the customer likely waives the statutory period.*

69. What is the statute of limitations period for a local government to sue to collect delinquent *wastewater* utility fees (that is, how long does a local government have to collect)?

The statute of limitations for collecting unpaid wastewater utility charges is three years.[14] G.S. 1-52(1). A local government may set a shorter limitations period by ordinance. The statute of limitations begins to run after the cause

---

govern the limitations period no matter what entity is being sued. North Carolina courts, however, have applied the two-year statutory period under G.S. 1-53 to actions against a local government arising out of a contract for the sale of water. *See* Jones v. Town of Angier, ___ N.C. App. ___, 638 S.E.2d 607 (2007). An argument can be made that if G.S. 1-52 governs the limitations period for contract actions against a local government arising out of the sale of water, the analogous provision for general contracts set forth in G.S. 1-53 should govern for all other contract actions arising out of the sale of water. A more likely interpretation of the three provisions, however, is that G.S. 25-2-725 applies to general contract actions arising out of the sale of water, whereas G.S. 1-53 provides for a limited exception where the action is against a unit of local government. This interpretation is consistent with the special treatment afforded units of local government throughout the statutes.

13. *See* Hargis v. City of Cookeville, 92 F. App'x 190 (6th Cir. Feb. 6, 2004) (rejecting argument that statutes of limitations had expired on the debt the city sought to collect for unpaid utility services because the customers entered into a written agreement to repay the utility bill, "thereby reaffirming the debt and waiving the affirmative defense of the statute of limitations").

14. *See* Rowan County Bd. of Educ. v. United States Gypsum Co., 332 N.C. 1, 418 S.E.2d 648 (1992) (stating that "[i]f the function is proprietary, time limitations do run against the State and its subdivisions unless the statute at issue expressly excludes the State").

of action has accrued. G.S. 1-15(a). In general, an action based on a contract accrues at the time of breach of the contract. A customer's failure to pay wastewater or solid waste utility fees by the periodic deadline specified by the local government constitutes a breach of the contract.

Note: The statute of limitations may be waived if a customer reaffirms the debt owed.[15] *For example, if a local government offers a payment plan option to delinquent customers and a customer enters into an agreement to repay the fees owed pursuant to the payment plan, the customer likely waives the statutory period.*

70. What is the statute of limitations period for a local government to sue to collect delinquent *solid waste* fees (that is, how long does a local government have to collect)?

The statutory period depends on how the fees are billed. A local government is authorized to bill for solid waste services along with the fees for other public enterprise services or to include the solid waste fees on the property tax bill.

If the fees are billed along with the fees for other public enterprise services, the statute of limitations for collecting unpaid charges is three years.[16] G.S. 1-52(1). A local government may set a shorter limitations period by ordinance. The statute of limitations begins to run after the cause of action has accrued. G.S. 1-15(a). In general, an action based on contract accrues at the time of breach of the contract. A customer's failure to pay solid waste fees by the periodic deadline specified by the local government constitutes a breach of the contract.

Alternatively, if the local government includes its solid waste services fees on the property tax bill and adopts an ordinance stating that the fees are payable in the same manner as property taxes and, in the case of nonpayment, collected

15. *See* Hargis v. City of Cookeville, 92 F. App'x 190 (6th Cir. Feb. 6, 2004) (rejecting argument that statutes of limitations had expired on the debt the city sought to collect for unpaid utility services because the customers entered into a written agreement to repay the utility bill, "thereby reaffirming the debt and waiving the affirmative defense of the statute of limitations").

16. *See* Rowan County Bd. of Educ. v. United States Gypsum Co., 332 N.C. 1, 418 S.E.2d 648 (1992) (stating that "[i]f the function is proprietary, time limitations do run against the State and its subdivisions unless the statute at issue expressly excludes the State").

in the same manner as delinquent real and personal property taxes, the statute of limitations is ten years from the date the fees become due. G.S. 105-378.

71. May a local government release delinquent public enterprise utility services accounts to a collection agency?

Yes. A county or city has broad authority to "contract with and appropriate money to any person, association, or corporation, in order to carry out any public purpose that the [unit] is authorized by law to engage in." G.S. 153A-449; G.S. 160A-20.1.[17] Although public enterprise billing information is not a public record, public disclosure is allowed if "necessary to assist the city, county, State, or public enterprise to maintain the integrity and quality of services it provides." G.S. 132-1.1(c)(2); *see also* G.S. 105A-15. Disclosing billing information to a collection agency for the purpose of collecting moneys owed to the utility is likely necessary to maintain the quality of services provided.

72. May a local government compromise a public enterprise utility services debt by extinguishing it without receiving full satisfaction of the amount owed?

Generally no. A local government likely has an obligation, rooted in general utility law, to collect any moneys owed.[18] Although North Carolina courts have not addressed this issue directly in the context of public enterprise utility services, in *Atlantic Coast Line Railroad v. West Paving Co.*[19] the North Carolina Supreme Court stated the following in addressing railroad rates:

---

17. *See also* G.S. 162A-88.1 (county water and sewer districts); G.S. 162A-6(11) (water and sewer authorities); G.S. 162A-36(1) and G.S. 162A-53(2) (metropolitan water districts); G.S. 162A-69(11) and G.S. 162A-73(2) (metropolitan sewer districts).

18. *See* Hous. Auth. of the County of King v. Northeast Lake Washington Sewer & Water Dist., 784 P.2d 1284, 1287 (Wash. Ct. App. 1990) (holding that statutory provision requiring water and sewer district to impose uniform charges for the same class of customer or service embodied a policy against rate discriminations and preferences); Chesapeake and Potomac Tel. Co. of Va. v. Bles, 243 S.E.2d 473 (Va. 1978) ("[I]t is apparent that to permit an undercharge, whether intentionally or inadvertently made, is to grant a [prohibited] preferential rebate to a customer. . . ."); Wisconsin Power & Light Co. v. Berlin Tanning & Mfg. Co., 83 N.W.2d 147 (Wis. 1957) (same).

19. 228 N.C. 94, 44 S.E.2d 523 (1947).

[u]nder well settled principles of law and in accord with the statutes enacted to prevent . . . discrimination among shippers, and to provide equal and impartial service to all alike, it was the duty of the plaintiff as a common carrier of freight to collect the full amount at the correct rate for transportation, and where a lawful charge therefore was negligently omitted, or rate misquoted, resulting in undercharge, the carrier was equally bound to exhaust all legal remedies to require payment in full of the proper charge.[20]

This case has been cited by other North Carolina courts as precedent for public enterprise utility services billing and collection practices.[21]

A local government's governing board, however, likely may adopt a policy proscribing debt collection efforts if the costs exceed the amount of debt owed. Such a policy would have to apply generally and would not support extinguishing an individual customer's debt on a case-by-case basis.[22]

73. May a local government assess late fees for delinquent public enterprise utility services fee payments?

Yes. The public enterprise statutes clearly authorize the assessment of late fee penalties. G.S. 160A-314; G.S. 153A-277. In *State of North Carolina ex rel. Utilities Commission v. North Carolina Consumers Council, Inc.*,[23] the North Carolina Court of Appeals described a *late fee charge* as "a device by which consumers are automatically classified to avoid discrimination." According to the court, assessing a late fee penalty "require[s] delinquent ratepayers to bear, as nearly as can be determined, the exact collection costs that result from their tardiness in paying their bills."

---

20. *Id.* at 97, 44 S.E.2d at 525. Some courts in other jurisdictions have distinguished between mistakes of fact and mistakes of law for purposes of applying the doctrine of equitable estoppel. For example, if there is a mistake in the rate charged, the customer is presumed to have knowledge of the rate. Thus a utility can collect the full amount owed even if it underbilled the customer. On the other hand, if the billing error involved a misread meter or a defective meter that was uniquely within the province of the utility to reasonably discover or prevent, a court might allow a claim of equitable estoppel. *See* Illinois Power Co. v. Champaign Asphalt Co., 310 N.E.2d 463 (Ill. Ct. App. 1974).

21. *See, e.g.,* City of Wilson v. Carolina Builders of Wilson, Inc., 94 N.C. App. 117, 379 S.E.2d 712 (1989).

22. *See generally* Roger D. Colton, *Protecting Against the Harms of the Mistaken Utility Undercharge*, 39 Wash. U. J. Urb. & Contemp. L. 99 (1991).

23. 18 N.C. App. 717, 198 S.E.2d 98 (1973).

If a local government includes its solid waste services fees on the property tax bill and adopts an ordinance stating that the fees are payable in the same manner as property taxes and, in the case of nonpayment, may be collected in any manner by which delinquent personal or real property taxes can be collected,[24] any delinquent fees are subject to the specific statutory interest penalties set forth in G.S. 105-360. The fees are due September 1 but are payable without interest through the following January 5.

74. Does a local government have to give the proceeds of late fee penalties to the local school administrative unit?

It depends on the nature of the underlying fee (whether it is actually a fee for service or an availability fee) and on the method by which the late fee penalties were adopted (whether by ordinance or resolution).

A local government "may provide for fines and penalties for violation of its ordinances and may secure injunctions and abatement orders to further insure compliance with its ordinances . . . ." G.S. 160A-175; G.S. 153A-123. Under Article IX, Section 7, of the N.C. Constitution, "the clear proceeds of all penalties and forfeitures and of all fines collected in the several counties for any breach of the penal laws of the state, shall belong to and remain in the several counties, and shall be faithfully appropriated and used exclusively for maintaining free public schools."

Generally, penalties collected for violations of local government ordinances, including late fee penalties, are civil in nature and do not implicate the penal laws of the state.[25] Violations of local government ordinances, however, have been made criminal by virtue of G.S. 14-4, which states that "if any person shall violate an ordinance of a county, city, town, or metropolitan sewerage . . . he shall be guilty of a Class 3 misdemeanor and shall be fined not more than five hundred dollars . . . ." Because of this, a local government must remit the moneys collected from any fines imposed for violation of a civil ordinance, including a fee ordinance, to the public schools.[26]

24. See Question 23.
25. Note that under some circumstances, violation of a local government ordinance also constitutes a violation of a state penal law. See Shavitz v. City of High Point, 177 N.C. App. 465, 630 S.E.2d 4 (2006) (holding that when city collected fines under its red light camera ordinance it was punishing motorists for violating a penal law of the state because failure to observe a red stoplight is illegal by virtue of a state statute).
26. See also Cauble v. City of Asheville, 301 N.C. 340, 271 S.E.2d 258 (1980).

A local government does have the option to opt out of the criminal enforcement remedy afforded by G.S. 14-4 if the governing board so provides in the ordinance. G.S. 160A-175; G.S. 153A-123. If the local government opts out of the criminal enforcement remedy, the fees imposed by the ordinance do not implicate the penal laws of the state and, thus, do not implicate the constitutional provision.

Moreover, the constitutional provision applies only to a violation of an ordinance. It is not implicated, for example, if failing to pay a public enterprise fee constitutes a violation of the contractual agreement between a local government and a customer. This is true because, although the fee schedule may be established by ordinance, the liability for payment of the public enterprise utility fee is triggered by the contractual agreement. Thus failure to pay the fee on time violates the contractual agreement, not the fee ordinance.

If a fee—such as a public enterprise utility services availability fee[27]—is imposed automatically by operation of the ordinance, however, failure to pay the fee violates the fee ordinance. In that case, unless the local government has opted out of the criminal remedy afforded by G.S. 14-4, any penalty imposed must be remitted to the public schools.

Finally, if a schedule of fees for public enterprise utility services—including availability fees—is adopted by resolution, a local government does not have to remit any of the moneys collected as late fees to the public schools.

75. May a local government assess a fee for a returned check or delayed rejection of debit payment for public enterprise utility services fees?

Yes. With the exception of certain solid waste services fees included on the property tax bill, a local government that accepts a check[28] as payment for public enterprise utility services fees may charge and collect a processing fee, not to exceed $25, for a check on which payment has been returned for insufficient funds or because the customer did not have an account at the bank.[29] G.S. 25-3-506; G.S. 25-3-104; G.S. 25-1-201(28) and (30).

---

27. For a detailed description of public enterprise utility services availability fees, see Questions 36 and 37.

28. A *check* is a draft payable on demand and drawn on a bank, or a cashier's check or teller's check.

29. Note that if a customer has multiple accounts for public enterprise utility services and issues a single check to cover fees due on more than one account, and the check is

If a local government includes its solid waste services fees on the property tax bill and adopts an ordinance stating that the fees are payable in the same manner as property taxes and, in the case of nonpayment, may be collected in any manner by which delinquent personal or real property taxes can be collected,[30] the unit may impose a penalty fee of $25 or 10 percent of the amount of the check or electronic invoice, whichever is greater, up to a maximum of $1,000.[31] G.S. 105-357(b)(2). The penalty is added to and collected in the same manner as the fees for which the check or electronic payment was given.

Note: If the local government employs a collection agency to collect the processing fee for a returned check, the collection agency must state the processing fee separately on its collection notice. Furthermore, the collection agency cannot collect or seek to collect from the customer any sum other than the actual amount of the returned check and the specified processing fee. G.S. 25-3-506.

Also, if the Administrative Office of the Courts authorizes a worthless check collection program pursuant to G.S. 14-107.2, the local district attorney may establish a program for the collection of worthless checks in cases that may be prosecuted under G.S. 14-107.

76. May a local government assess a late fee for a delinquent public enterprise utility services fee payment if a customer issues payment on or before the payment deadline but the customer's check is returned or debit payment is rejected because of insufficient funds?

Yes. If a check is returned or debit payment is rejected because of insufficient funds, a local government may assess a late fee penalty on the customer even if the original payment occurred before the payment deadline.

---

returned for insufficient funds, the local government unit may assess only a single returned check fee, for up to $25. The unit may assess a late fee penalty on each account that is delinquent, though.

30. See Question 82.

31. The "penalty does not apply if the local government finds that, when the check or electronic funds transfer was presented for payment, the drawer of the check or transferor of funds had sufficient funds in an account at a financial institution in this State to make the payment and, by inadvertence, the drawer of the check or transferor of the funds failed to draw the check or initiate a transfer on the account that had sufficient funds." G.S. 105-357(b)(2).

77. If a customer is delinquent in public enterprise utility services fee payments, is a local government required to apply any deposit or security fees collected when the account was opened[32] toward the amount owed before resorting to other authorized collection remedies?

No. A local government may resort to any remedies authorized by law for collection of delinquent public enterprise utility services fees. G.S. 153A-277(b); G.S. 160A-314(b). For example, a unit is not obligated to apply a deposit or security fee toward any amounts owed before discontinuing service to a property or premises, even if the deposit or security fee moneys exceed the amounts owed.[33] A local government is entitled to require that the deposit or security fee be kept intact during the continuance of the service relationship.

As a matter of practice, a local government should inform a customer at the time the deposit or security fee is rendered whether or not it will be applied to delinquent public enterprise utility services fees before discontinuation of service.[34]

78. If a potential customer pays a tap fee deposit to reserve the right to connect to the local government's water or wastewater system at a later date but does not connect, may the local government apply the deposit to delinquent availability fees owed by the potential customer?

No, unless there is some language in the tap fee agreement, or in the ordinance or resolution establishing the tap fee, stating that the tap fee amount may be forfeited if any availability fees (or other public enterprise utility fees) are delinquent.

---

32. See Question 3.

33. *See, e.g.,* Community Natural Gas Co. v. Moss, 55 S.W.2d 224 (Ct. Civ. App. Tex. 1932); Hewsey v. Queens Borough Gas & Elec. Co., 93 N.Y.S. 1114 (N.Y. App. Term 1905).

34. For example, a local government may wish to include a statement on the contract for services or on the deposit receipt along the lines of the following: "This deposit is nontransferable, non–interest bearing, and will not be considered as partial payment of any bill where service is continued."

79. May a local government apply a deposit or security fee to delinquent public enterprise utility fees if the customer has filed for bankruptcy?

Yes. Under federal bankruptcy law, a local government may recover or set off against a pre-petition utility services deposit or security fee provided to the unit by the debtor for water and wastewater services (and possible solid waste services) without notice or leave of the bankruptcy court. 11 U.S.C. § 366(c) (4) (2007).

80. If a local government includes the fees for solid waste services on the property tax bill, may the local government provide a discount for payment of the fees prior to the due date?

Yes. If a local government includes its solid waste services fees on the property tax bill and adopts an ordinance stating that the fees are payable in the same manner as property taxes and, in the case of nonpayment, may be collected in any manner by which delinquent personal or real property taxes may be collected, the unit may apply the same prepayment discounts it applies to early property tax payments. State law prescribes some conditions for establishing the prepayment discounts, which are set forth in G.S. 105-360(c).

81. If a local government includes the fees for solid waste services on the property tax bill, may the local government charge interest on delinquent fees according to G.S. 105-360?

Yes. If a local government includes its solid waste services fees on the property tax bill and adopts an ordinance stating that the fees are payable in the same manner as property taxes and, in the case of nonpayment, may be collected in any manner by which delinquent personal or real property taxes may be collected, any delinquent fees are subject to the specific statutory interest penalties set forth in G.S. 105-360. The fees are due on September 1 but are payable without interest through the following January 5.[35]

---

35. When January 5 falls on a Saturday, Sunday, or holiday, the property owner may pay the fees without interest on the next business day.

82. If a local government includes the fees for solid waste services on the property tax bill, what remedies does the unit have to collect delinquent fees?

If a local government includes its solid waste services fees on the property tax bill and adopts an ordinance stating that the fees are payable in the same manner as property taxes and, in the case of nonpayment, may be collected in any manner by which delinquent personal or real property taxes may be collected, the fees are a lien on the underlying property served. The lien attaches on the date as of which the real property is to be listed under G.S. 105-285. The lien has the same priority status as a lien for real or personal property taxes; it is superior to all other liens and rights except previously recorded liens for state taxes, regardless of whether the other liens were acquired before the lien for the delinquent fees. G.S. 105-356(a)(1) & (2). Furthermore, once the lien has attached to real property, its priority is not affected by transfer of title, by death, or by receivership of the property owner. G.S. 105-356(a)(3). A local government must follow the procedures set forth in G.S. 105-369, G.S. 105-374, and G.S. 105-375 for enforcement of the lien against the real property. A unit also may employ the remedies of levy and attachment and garnishment against personal property to enforce the collection of delinquent fees.[36] G.S. 105-366; G.S. 105-367; G.S. 105-368. For purposes of utilizing these remedies to collect the delinquent fees, the *taxpayer* is defined as the owner of the property as of January 1 of the calendar year in which the fiscal year for which the solid waste fees are assessed opens.

Of course, a local government also may discontinue solid waste services to a delinquent customer according to its adopted policies and procedures in order to compel payment of the fees owed.[37]

---

36. For a detailed description of the collection process for delinquent property taxes, see Shea Riggsbee Denning, *The Property Tax, in* COUNTY AND MUNICIPAL GOVERNMENT IN NORTH CAROLINA 19–25 (David M. Lawrence ed., 2006).

37. See Question 48.

83. If a local government includes the fees for solid waste services on the property tax bill, does a delinquent customer have the same remedies as a delinquent taxpayer?

Likely yes. If a local government includes its solid waste services fees on the property tax bill and adopts an ordinance stating that the fees are payable in the same manner as property taxes and, in the case of nonpayment, may be collected in any manner by which delinquent personal or real property taxes may be collected, a delinquent customer likely may assert a defense to the enforcement of the fee assessed according to the procedures set forth in G.S. 105-381.

VI Miscellaneous

84. May a local government sponsor a public assistance program to aid customers who cannot pay their public enterprise utility services fees?

Yes. A local government has broad authority to sponsor programs addressing the welfare needs of its low- or moderate income residents. G.S. 160A-456; G.S. 153A-376. This authority likely extends to establishing a public assistance program to aid customers in paying public enterprise utility services fees. The local government must contract with a private organization to run the public assistance subsidy or rebate program or establish the program as a general fund activity. It may not provide public assistance by reducing the public enterprise utility fees directly.[1]

85. May a local government establish a payment plan for public enterprise utility services fees owed?

Yes. A local government can establish a payment plan for delinquent public enterprise utility services fees. It likely cannot extinguish outstanding debt, however.[2]

---

1. A local government may not establish a utility rate schedule according to income levels or ability to pay, because redistribution of income is not a valid utility rate-making function. *See* Kara A. Millonzi, *Lawful Discrimination in Utility Ratemaking, Part 1: Classifying Customers within Territorial Boundaries*, LOCAL FINANCE BULLETIN 33, at 6 (Oct. 2006).

2. See Question 72.

86. What is the statute of limitations period for a public enterprise utility customer to sue a local government to collect for any public enterprise service overbillings?

The statute of limitations for recovering against a local government for overbilling for public enterprise utility services is two years.[3] G.S. 1-53(1). The same statute of limitations applies to any suit against the local government arising from the contractual relationship with the public enterprise utility services customer.

87. Are there any legal consequences to an individual who connects to a water meter, or reconnects to a water meter after service has been discontinued by the local government for nonpayment, without prior authorization from the local government?

Yes. G.S. 14-151.1 makes it unlawful for any unauthorized person to alter, tamper with, or bypass a meter that has been installed for the purpose of measuring the use of water or to knowingly use water passing through a tampered meter supplied by the utility provider for the purpose of measuring and registering the amount of water consumed. The statute also prohibits any unauthorized person from reconnecting water connections or otherwise turning back on water service when it has been lawfully disconnected or turned off by the provider of the utility service.

If an individual is found in a civil action to have violated any provision of G.S. 14-151.1, he or she is liable to the water supplier in triple the amount of losses and damages, up to a maximum of $500.[4]

---

3. *See* Jones v. Town of Angier, ___ N.C. App. ___, 638 S.E.2d 607 (2007).

4. Note that any penalty amount collected by a local government for violation of G.S. 14-151.1 likely must be distributed to the local school district in compliance with Article IX, Section 7 of the North Carolina Constitution. See Question 74.

Appendix

This appendix contains the text of the North Carolina public enterprise statutes. References to G.S. 153A apply to counties and references to G.S. 160A apply to municipalities. The statutory provisions are current through June 2008.

Counties

§ 153A-274. Public enterprise defined.

As used in this Article, "public enterprise" includes:

(1)　Water supply and distribution systems.

(2)　Wastewater collection, treatment, and disposal systems of all types, including septic tank systems or other on-site collection or disposal facilities or systems.

(3)　Solid waste collection and disposal systems and facilities.

(4)　Airports.

(5)　Off-street parking facilities.

(6)　Public transportation systems.

(7)　Stormwater management programs designed to protect water quality by controlling the level of pollutants in, and the quantity and flow of, stormwater and structural and natural stormwater and drainage systems of all types. (1965, c. 370; 1957, c. 266, s. 3; 1961, c. 514, s. 1; c. 1001, s. 1; 1971, c. 568; 1973, c. 822, s. 1; c. 1214; 1977, c. 514, s. 1; 1979, c. 619, s. 1; 1989, c. 643, s. 2; 1991 (Reg. Sess., 1992), c. 944, s. 13; 2000-70, s. 1.)

§ 153A-275. Authority to operate public enterprises.

(a)   A county may acquire, lease as lessor or lessee, construct, establish, enlarge, improve, extend, maintain, own, operate, and contract for the operation of public enterprises in order to furnish services to the county and its citizens. A county may acquire, construct, establish, enlarge, improve, maintain, own, and operate outside its borders any public enterprise.

(b)   A county may adopt adequate and reasonable rules to protect and regulate a public enterprise belonging to or operated by it. The rules shall be adopted by ordinance, shall apply to the public enterprise system both within and outside the county, and may be enforced with the remedies available under any provision of law. (1955, c. 370; 1957, c. 266, s. 3; 1961, c. 514, s. 1; c. 1001, s. 1; 1967, c. 462; 1971, c. 568; 1973, c. 822, s. 1; 1991 (Reg. Sess., 1992), c. 836, s. 2.)

§ 153A-276. Financing public enterprises.

Subject to the restrictions, limitations, procedures, and regulations otherwise provided by law, a county may finance the cost of a public enterprise by levying taxes, borrowing money, and appropriating any other revenues, and by accepting and administering gifts and grants from any source. (1973, c. 822, s. 1.)

§ 153A-277. Authority to fix and enforce rates.

(a)   A county may establish and revise from time to time schedules of rents, rates, fees, charges, and penalties for the use of or the services furnished by a public enterprise. Schedules of rents, rates, fees, charges, and penalties may vary for the same class of service in different areas of the county and may vary according to classes of service, and different schedules may be adopted for services provided outside of the county. A county may include a fee relating to subsurface discharge wastewater management systems and services on the property tax bill for the real property where the system for which the fee is imposed is located.

(a1)   (1)   Before it establishes or revises a schedule of rates, fees, charges, or penalties for stormwater management programs and structural and natural stormwater and drainage systems under this section, the board of commissioners shall hold a public hearing on the matter. A notice of the hearing shall be given at least once in a newspaper having general circulation in the area, not less than seven days before the public hearing. The hearing may be held concurrently with the public hearing on the proposed budget ordinance.

(2) The fees established under this subsection must be made applicable throughout the area of the county outside municipalities. Schedules of rates, fees, charges, and penalties for providing stormwater management programs and structural and natural stormwater and drainage system service may vary according to whether the property served is residential, commercial, or industrial property, the property's use, the size of the property, the area of impervious surfaces on the property, the quantity and quality of the runoff from the property, the characteristics of the watershed into which stormwater from the property drains, and other factors that affect the stormwater drainage system. Rates, fees, and charges imposed under this subsection may not exceed the county's cost of providing a stormwater management program and a structural and natural stormwater and drainage system. The county's cost of providing a stormwater management program and a structural and natural stormwater and drainage system includes any costs necessary to assure that all aspects of stormwater quality and quantity are managed in accordance with federal and State laws, regulations, and rules.

(3) No stormwater utility fee may be levied under this subsection whenever two or more units of local government operate separate stormwater management programs or separate structural and natural stormwater and drainage system services in the same area within a county. However, two or more units of local government may allocate among themselves the functions, duties, powers, and responsibilities for jointly operating a stormwater management program and structural and natural stormwater and drainage system service in the same area within a county, provided that only one unit may levy a fee for the service within the joint service area. For purposes of this subsection, a unit of local government shall include a regional authority providing stormwater management programs and structural and natural stormwater and drainage system services.

(b)   A county may collect delinquent accounts by any remedy provided by law for collecting and enforcing private debts, and may specify by ordinance the order in which partial payments are to be applied among the various enterprise services covered by a bill for the services. A county may also discontinue service to a customer whose account remains delinquent for more than 10 days. If a delinquent customer is not the owner of the premises to which the services are delivered, the payment of the delinquent account may not be required before providing services at the request of a new and different tenant or occupant of the premises. If water or sewer services are discontinued for delinquency, it is unlawful for a person other than a duly authorized agent or employee of the county to reconnect the premises to the water or sewer system.

(c)   Rents, rates, fees, charges, and penalties for enterprisory services are in no case a lien upon the property or premises served and, except as provided in subsection (d) of this section, are legal obligations of the person contracting for them, provided that no contract shall be necessary in the case of structural and natural stormwater and drainage systems.

(d)   Rents, rates, fees, charges, and penalties for enterprisory services are legal obligations of the owner of the property or premises served when:

> (1)   The property or premises is leased or rented to more than one tenant and services rendered to more than one tenant are measured by the same meter; or
>
> (2)   Charges made for use of a sewerage system are billed separately from charges made for the use of a water distribution system. (1961, c. 1001, s. 1; 1973, c. 822, s. 1; 1991, c. 591, s. 2; 1991 (Reg. Sess., 1992), c. 932, s. 3; c. 1007, s. 45; 2000-70, s. 2.)

§ 153A-278. Joint provision of enterprisory services.

Two or more counties, cities, or other units of local government may cooperate in the exercise of any power granted by this Article according to the procedures and provisions of Chapter 160A, Article 20, Part 1. (1961, c. 1001, s. 1; 1973, c. 822, s. 1.)

§ 153A-279. Limitations on rail transportation liability.

(a)   As used in this section:

> (1)   "Claim" means a claim, action, suit, or request for damages, whether compensatory, punitive, or otherwise, made by any person or entity against:

a. The County, a railroad, or an operating rights railroad; or

b. An officer, director, trustee, employee, parent, subsidiary, or affiliated corporation as defined in G.S. 105-130.6, or agent of: the County, a railroad, or an operating rights railroad.

(2) "Operating rights railroad" means a railroad corporation or railroad company that, prior to January 1, 2001, was granted operating rights by a State-Owned Railroad Company or operated over the property of a State-owned railroad company under a claim of right over or adjacent to facilities used by or on behalf of the County.

(3) "Passenger rail services" means the transportation of rail passengers by or on behalf of the County and all services performed by a railroad pursuant to a contract with the County in connection with the transportation of rail passengers, including, but not limited to, the operation of trains; the use of right-of-way, trackage, public or private roadway and rail crossings, equipment, or station areas or appurtenant facilities; the design, construction, reconstruction, operation, or maintenance of rail-related equipment, tracks, and any appurtenant facilities; or the provision of access rights over or adjacent to lines owned by the County or a railroad, or otherwise occupied by the County or a railroad, pursuant to charter grant, fee-simple deed, lease, easement, license, trackage rights, or other form of ownership or authorized use.

(4) "Railroad" means a railroad corporation or railroad company, including a State-Owned Railroad Company as defined in G.S. 124-11, that has entered into any contracts or operating agreements of any kind with the County concerning passenger rail services.

(b) Contracts Allocating Financial Responsibility Authorized. – The County may contract with any railroad to allocate financial responsibility for passenger rail services claims, including, but not limited to, the execution of indemnity agreements, notwithstanding any other statutory, common law, public policy, or other prohibition against same, and regardless of the nature of the claim or the conduct giving rise to such claim.

(c) Insurance Required. –

    (1)   If the County enters into any contract authorized by subsection (b) of this section, the contract shall require the County to secure and maintain, upon and after the commencement of the operation of trains by or on behalf of the county, a liability insurance policy covering the liability of the parties to the contract, a State-Owned Railroad Company as defined in G.S. 124-11 that owns or claims an interest in any real property subject to the contract, and any operating rights railroad for all claims for property damage, personal injury, bodily injury, and death arising out of or related to passenger rail services. The policy shall name the parties to the contract, a State-Owned Railroad Company as defined in G.S. 124-11 that owns or claims an interest in any real property subject to the contract, and any operating rights railroad as named insureds and shall have policy limits of not less than two hundred million dollars ($200,000,000) per single accident or incident, and may include a self-insured retention in an amount of not more than five million dollars ($5,000,000).

    (2)   If the County does not enter into any contract authorized by subsection (b) of this section, upon and after the commencement of the operation of trains by or on behalf of the County, the County shall secure and maintain a liability insurance policy, with policy limits and a self-insured retention consistent with subdivision (1) of this subsection, for all claims for property damage, personal injury, bodily injury, and death arising out of or related to passenger rail services.

(d) Liability Limit. – The aggregate liability of the County, the parties to the contract or contracts authorized by subsection (b) of this section, a State-Owned Railroad Company as defined in G.S. 124-11, and any operating rights railroad for all claims arising from a single accident or incident related to passenger rail services for property damage, personal injury, bodily injury, and death is limited to two hundred million dollars ($200,000,000) per single accident or incident or to any proceeds available under any insurance policy secured pursuant to subsection (c) of this section, whichever is greater.

(e) Effect on Other Laws. – This section shall not affect the damages that may be recovered under the Federal Employers' Liability Act, 45 U.S.C. § 51, et seq., (1908); or under Article 1 of Chapter 97 of the General Statutes.

(f)   Applicability. – This section shall apply only to counties that have entered into a transit governance interlocal agreement with, among other local governments, a city with a population of more than 500,000 persons. (2002-78, s. 2.)

§ 153A-280. Public enterprise improvements.

(a)   Authorization. – A county may contract with a developer or property owner, or with a private party who is under contract with the developer or property owner, for public enterprise improvements that are adjacent or ancillary to a private land development project. Such a contract shall allow the county to reimburse the private party for costs associated with the design and construction of improvements that are in addition to those required by the county's land development regulations. Such a contract is not subject to Article 8 of Chapter 143 of the General Statutes if the public cost will not exceed two hundred fifty thousand dollars ($250,000) and the county determines that: (i) the public cost will not exceed the estimated cost of providing for those improvements through either eligible force account qualified labor or through a public contract let pursuant to Article 8 of Chapter 143 of the General Statutes; or (ii) the coordination of separately constructed improvements would be impracticable. A county may enact ordinances and policies setting forth the procedures, requirements, and terms for agreements authorized by this section.

(b)   Property Acquisition. – The improvements may be constructed on property owned or acquired by the private party or on property owned or acquired by the county. The private party may assist the county in obtaining easements in favor of the county from private property owners on those properties that will be involved in or affected by the project. The contract between the county and the private party may be entered into before the acquisition of any real property necessary to the project. (2005-426, s. 8(e).)

§ 153A-281. Reserved for future codification purposes.

§ 153A-282. Reserved for future codification purposes.

Part 2. Special Provisions for Water and Sewer Services.

§ 153A-283. Nonliability for failure to furnish water or sewer services.

In no case may a county be held liable for damages for failure to furnish water or sewer services. (1961, c. 1001, s. 1; 1973, c. 822, s. 1.)

§ 153A-284. Power to require connections.

A county may require the owner of developed property on which there are situated one or more residential dwelling units or commercial establishments located so as to be served by a water line or sewer collection line owned, leased as lessee, or operated by the county or on behalf of the county to connect the owner's premises with the water or sewer line and may fix charges for these connections. In the case of improved property that would qualify for the issuance of a building permit for the construction of one or more residential dwelling units or commercial establishments and where the county has installed water or sewer lines or a combination thereof directly available to the property, the county may require payment of a periodic availability charge, not to exceed the minimum periodic service charge for properties that are connected. (1963, c. 985, s. 1; 1965, c. 969, s. 2; 1973, c. 822, s. 1; 1979, c. 619, s. 13; 1995, c. 511, s. 3.)

§ 153A-285: Repealed by Session Laws 1993, c. 348, s. 4.

§ 153A-286. Law with respect to riparian rights not changed.

Nothing in this Article changes or modifies existing common or statute law with respect to the relative rights of riparian owners or others concerning the use of or disposal of water in the streams of North Carolina. (1961, c. 1001, s. 1; 1973, c. 822, s. 1.)

§ 153A-287: Repealed by Session Laws 1993, c. 348, s. 5.

§ 153A-288. Venue for actions by riparian owners.

Any riparian owner alleging injury as a result of an act taken pursuant to this Article by a county or city acting jointly or by a joint agency may maintain an action for relief against the act (i) in the county where the land of the riparian owner lies, (ii) in the county taking the action, or (iii) in any county in which the city or joint agency is located or operates. (1961, c. 1001, s. 1; 1973, c. 822, s. 1.)

§ 153A-289. Reserved for future codification purposes.

§ 153A-290. Reserved for future codification purposes.

Part 3. Special Provisions for Solid Waste Collection and Disposal.

§ 153A-291. Cooperation between the Department of Transportation and any county in establishing or operating solid waste disposal facilities.

A county and the Department of Transportation may enter into an agreement under which the Department of Transportation will make available to the county the use of equipment and prison and other labor in order to establish or operate solid waste disposal facilities within the county. The county shall reimburse the Department of Transportation for the cost of providing the equipment and labor. The agreement shall specify the work to be done thereunder and shall set forth the basis for reimbursement. (1967, c. 707; 1973, c. 507, s. 5; c. 822, s. 1; 1977, c. 464, s. 34.)

§ 153A-292. County collection and disposal facilities.

(a)   The board of county commissioners of any county may establish and operate solid waste collection and disposal facilities in areas outside the corporate limits of a city. The board may by ordinance regulate the use of a disposal facility provided by the county, the nature of the solid wastes disposed of in a facility, and the method of disposal. The board may contract with any city, individual, or privately owned corporation to collect and dispose of solid waste in the area. Counties and cities may establish and operate joint collection and disposal facilities. A joint agreement shall be in writing and executed by the governing bodies of the participating units of local government.

(b)   The board of county commissioners may impose a fee for the collection of solid waste. The fee may not exceed the costs of collection.

The board of county commissioners may impose a fee for the use of a disposal facility provided by the county. The fee for use may not exceed the cost of operating the facility and may be imposed only on those who use the facility. The fee for use may vary based on the amount, characteristics, and form of recyclable materials present in solid waste brought to the facility for disposal. A county may not impose a fee for the use of a disposal facility on a city located in the county or a contractor or resident of the city unless the fee is based on a schedule that applies uniformly throughout the county.

The board of county commissioners may impose a fee for the availability of a disposal facility provided by the county. A fee for availability may not exceed the cost of providing the facility and may be imposed on all improved property in the county that benefits from the availability of the facility. A county may not impose an availability fee on property whose solid waste is collected by a county, a city, or a private contractor for a fee if the fee imposed by a county, a city, or a private contractor for the collection of solid waste includes a charge for the availability and use of a disposal facility provided by the county. Property served by a private contractor who disposes of solid waste collected from the property in a disposal facility provided by a private contractor that provides the same services as those provided by the county disposal facility is not considered to benefit from a disposal facility provided by the county and is not subject to a fee imposed by the county for the availability of a disposal facility provided by the county. To the extent that the services provided by the county disposal facility differ from the services provided by the disposal facility provided by a private contractor in the same county, the county may charge an availability fee to cover the costs of the additional services provided by the county disposal facility.

In determining the costs of providing and operating a disposal facility, a county may consider solid waste management costs incidental to a county's handling and disposal of solid waste at its disposal facility, including the costs of the methods of solid waste management specified in G.S. 130A-309.04(a) of the Solid Waste Management Act of 1989. A fee for the availability or use of a disposal facility may be based on the combined costs of the different disposal facilities provided by the county.

(c)   The board of county commissioners may use any suitable vacant land owned by the county for the site of a disposal facility, subject to the permit requirements of Article 9 of Chapter 130A of the General Statutes. If the county does not own suitable vacant land for a disposal facility, it may acquire suitable land by purchase or condemnation. The board may erect a gate across a highway that leads directly to a disposal facility operated by the county. The gate may be erected at or in close proximity to the boundary of the disposal facility. The county shall pay the cost of erecting and maintaining the gate.

(d), (e) Repealed by Session Laws 1991, c. 652, s. 1.

(f)   This section does not prohibit a county from providing aid to low-income persons to pay all or part of the cost of solid waste management services for those persons. (1961, c. 514, s. 1; 1971, c. 568; 1973, c. 535; c. 822,

s. 2; 1981, c. 919, s. 22; 1989 (Reg. Sess., 1990), c. 1009, s. 3; 1991, c. 652, s. 1; 1995 (Reg. Sess., 1996), c. 594, s. 27; 2007-550, s. 10(a).)

§ 153A-293. (See editor's note) Collection of fees for solid waste disposal facilities and solid waste collection services.

A county may adopt an ordinance providing that any fee imposed under G.S. 153A-292 may be billed with property taxes, may be payable in the same manner as property taxes, and, in the case of nonpayment, may be collected in any manner by which delinquent personal or real property taxes can be collected. If an ordinance states that delinquent fees can be collected in the same manner as delinquent real property taxes, the fees are a lien on the real property described on the bill that includes the fee. (1989, c. 591; 1989 (Reg. Sess., 1990), c. 905, c. 938, c. 940, c. 974, c. 1017; 1991, c. 652, s. 2; 1991 (Reg. Sess., 1992), c. 1007, s. 26.)

§ 153A-294. Solid waste defined.

As used in this Article, "solid waste" means nonhazardous solid waste, that is, solid waste as defined in G.S. 130A-290 but not including hazardous waste. (1991 (Reg. Sess., 1992), c. 1013, s. 4.)

§§ G.S. 153A-295 through 153A-299. Reserved for future codification purposes.

Part 4. Long Term Contracts for Disposal of Soild Waste.

§§ 153A-299.1 through 153A-299.6: Repealed by Session Laws 1991 (Regular Session, 1992), c. 1013, 5.

Municipalities

§ 160A-311. Public enterprise defined.

As used in this Article, the term "public enterprise" includes:

(1)   Electric power generation, transmission, and distribution systems.

(2)   Water supply and distribution systems.

(3)   Wastewater collection, treatment, and disposal systems of all types, including septic tank systems or other on-site collection or disposal facilities or systems.

(4)   Gas production, storage, transmission, and distribution systems, where systems shall also include the purchase or lease of natural gas fields and natural gas reserves, the purchase of natural gas supplies, and the surveying, drilling and any other activities related to the exploration for natural gas, whether within the State or without.

(5)   Public transportation systems.

(6)   Solid waste collection and disposal systems and facilities.

(7)   Cable television systems.

(8)   Off-street parking facilities and systems.

(9)   Airports.

(10)   Stormwater management programs designed to protect water quality by controlling the level of pollutants in, and the quantity and flow of, stormwater and structural and natural stormwater and drainage systems of all types. (1971, c. 698, s. 1; 1975, c. 549, s. 2; c. 821, s. 3; 1977, c. 514, s. 2; 1979, c. 619, s. 2; 1989, c. 643, s. 5; 1991 (Reg. Sess., 1992), c. 944, s. 14; 2000-70, s. 3.)

§ 160A-312. Authority to operate public enterprises.

(a)   A city shall have authority to acquire, construct, establish, enlarge, improve, maintain, own, operate, and contract for the operation of any or all of the public enterprises as defined in this Article to furnish services to the city and its citizens. Subject to Part 2 of this Article, a city may acquire, construct, establish, enlarge, improve, maintain, own, and operate any public enterprise outside its corporate limits, within reasonable limitations, but in no case shall a city be held liable for damages to those outside the corporate limits for failure to furnish any public enterprise service.

(b) A city shall have full authority to protect and regulate any public enterprise system belonging to or operated by it by adequate and reasonable rules. The rules shall be adopted by ordinance, shall apply to the public enterprise system both within and outside the corporate limits of the city, and may be enforced with the remedies available under any provision of law.

(c) A city may operate that part of a gas system involving the purchase and/or lease of natural gas fields, natural gas reserves and natural gas supplies and the surveying, drilling or any other activities related to the exploration for natural gas, in a partnership or joint venture arrangement with natural gas utilities and private enterprise. (1971, c. 698, s. 1; 1973, c. 426, s. 51; 1975, c. 821, s. 5; 1979, 2nd Sess., c. 1247, s. 29; 1991 (Reg. Sess., 1992), c. 836, s. 1.)

§ 160A-313. Financing public enterprise.

Subject to the restrictions, limitations, procedures, and regulations otherwise provided by law, a city shall have full authority to finance the cost of any public enterprise by levying taxes, borrowing money, and appropriating any other revenues therefor, and by accepting and administering gifts and grants from any source on behalf thereof. (1971, c. 698, s. 1.)

§ 160A-314. Authority to fix and enforce rates.

(a) A city may establish and revise from time to time schedules of rents, rates, fees, charges, and penalties for the use of or the services furnished by any public enterprise. Schedules of rents, rates, fees, charges, and penalties may vary according to classes of service, and different schedules may be adopted for services provided outside the corporate limits of the city.

(a1) (1) Before it establishes or revises a schedule of rates, fees, charges, or penalties for stormwater management programs and structural and natural stormwater and drainage systems under this section, the city council shall hold a public hearing on the matter. A notice of the hearing shall be given at least once in a newspaper having general circulation in the area, not less than seven days before the public hearing. The hearing may be held concurrently with the public hearing on the proposed budget ordinance.

(2) The fees established under this subsection must be made applicable throughout the area of the city. Schedules of rates, fees, charges, and penalties for providing stormwater management programs and structural and natural stormwater

and drainage system service may vary according to whether the property served is residential, commercial, or industrial property, the property's use, the size of the property, the area of impervious surfaces on the property, the quantity and quality of the runoff from the property, the characteristics of the watershed into which stormwater from the property drains, and other factors that affect the stormwater drainage system. Rates, fees, and charges imposed under this subsection may not exceed the city's cost of providing a stormwater management program and a structural and natural stormwater and drainage system. The city's cost of providing a stormwater management program and a structural and natural stormwater and drainage system includes any costs necessary to assure that all aspects of stormwater quality and quantity are managed in accordance with federal and State laws, regulations, and rules.

(3) No stormwater utility fee may be levied under this subsection whenever two or more units of local government operate separate stormwater management programs or separate structural and natural stormwater and drainage system services in the same area within a county. However, two or more units of local government may allocate among themselves the functions, duties, powers, and responsibilities for jointly operating a stormwater management program and structural and natural stormwater and drainage system service in the same area within a county, provided that only one unit may levy a fee for the service within the joint service area. For purposes of this subsection, a unit of local government shall include a regional authority providing stormwater management programs and structural and natural stormwater and drainage system services.

(a2) A fee for the use of a disposal facility provided by the city may vary based on the amount, characteristics, and form of recyclable materials present in solid waste brought to the facility for disposal. This section does not prohibit a city from providing aid to low-income persons to pay all or part of the cost of solid waste management services for those persons.

(b)   A city shall have power to collect delinquent accounts by any remedy provided by law for collecting and enforcing private debts, and may specify by ordinance the order in which partial payments are to be applied among the various enterprise services covered by a bill for the services. A city may also discontinue service to any customer whose account remains delinquent for more than 10 days. When service is discontinued for delinquency, it shall be unlawful for any person other than a duly authorized agent or employee of the city to do any act that results in a resumption of services. If a delinquent customer is not the owner of the premises to which the services are delivered, the payment of the delinquent account may not be required before providing services at the request of a new and different tenant or occupant of the premises, but this restriction shall not apply when the premises are occupied by two or more tenants whose services are measured by the same meter.

(c)   Except as provided in subsection (d) of this section and G.S. 160A-314.1, rents, rates, fees, charges, and penalties for enterprisory services shall be legal obligations of the person contracting for them, and shall in no case be a lien upon the property or premises served, provided that no contract shall be necessary in the case of structural and natural stormwater and drainage systems.

(d)   Rents, rates, fees, charges, and penalties for enterprisory services shall be legal obligations of the owner of the premises served when:

> (1)   The property or premises is leased or rented to more than one tenant and services rendered to more than one tenant are measured by the same meter.
>
> (2)   Charges made for use of a sewage system are billed separately from charges made for the use of a water distribution system.

(e)   Nothing in this section shall repeal any portion of any city charter inconsistent herewith. (1971, c. 698, s. 1; 1991, c. 591, s. 1; c. 652, s. 4; 1991 (Reg. Sess., 1992), c. 1007, s. 46; 1995 (Reg. Sess., 1996), c. 594, s. 28; 2000-70, s. 4.)

§ 160A-314.1. Availability fees for solid waste disposal facilities; collection of any solid waste fees.

(a)   In addition to a fee that a city may impose for collecting solid waste or for using a disposal facility, a city may impose a fee for the availability of a disposal facility provided by the city. A fee for availability may not exceed the cost of providing the facility and may be imposed on all improved property in the city that benefits from the availability of the facility. A city may not impose an availability fee on property whose solid waste is collected by a county, a city, or a private contractor for a fee if the fee imposed by a county, a city, or a private contractor for the collection of solid waste includes a charge for the availability and use of a disposal facility provided by the city. Property served by a private contractor who disposes of solid waste collected from the property in a disposal facility provided by a private contractor that provides the same services as those provided by the city disposal facility is not considered to benefit from a disposal facility provided by the city and is not subject to a fee imposed by the city for the availability of a disposal facility provided by the city. To the extent that the services provided by the city disposal facility differ from the services provided by the disposal facility provided by a private contractor in the same city, the city may charge an availability fee to cover the costs of the additional services provided by the city disposal facility.

In determining the costs of providing and operating a disposal facility, a city may consider solid waste management costs incidental to a city's handling and disposal of solid waste at its disposal facility. A fee for the availability or use of a disposal facility may be based on the combined costs of the different disposal facilities provided by the city.

(b)   A city may adopt an ordinance providing that any fee imposed under subsection (a) or under G.S. 160A-314 for collecting or disposing of solid waste may be billed with property taxes, may be payable in the same manner as property taxes, and, in the case of nonpayment, may be collected in any manner by which delinquent personal or real property taxes can be collected. If an ordinance states that delinquent fees can be collected in the same manner as delinquent real property taxes, the fees are a lien on the real property described on the bill that includes the fee. (1991, c. 652, s. 5; 2007-550, s. 10(b).)

§ 160A-315. Billing and collecting agents for certain sewer systems.

Any city that maintains and operates a sewage collection and disposal system but does not maintain and operate a water distribution system is authorized to contract with the owner or operator of the water distribution system operating within the area served by the city sewer system to act as the billing and collection agent of the city for any charges, rents, or penalties imposed by the city for sewer services. (1933, c. 322, s. 1; 1941, c. 106; 1961, c. 1074; 1971, c. 698, s. 1.)

§ 160A-316. Independent water companies to supply information.

The owner or operator of any independent or private water distribution system operating within a city that maintains and operates a sewage collection and disposal system shall furnish to the city upon request copies of water meter readings and any other water consumption records and data that the city may require to bill and collect its sewer rents and charges. The city shall pay the reasonable cost of supplying this information. (1933, c. 322, s. 1; 1941, c. 106; 1961, c. 1074; 1971, c. 698, s. 1.)

§ 160A-317. Power to require connections to water or sewer service and the use of solid waste collection services.

(a) Connections. – A city may require an owner of developed property on which there are situated one or more residential dwelling units or commercial establishments located within the city limits and within a reasonable distance of any water line or sewer collection line owned, leased as lessee, or operated by the city or on behalf of the city to connect the owner's premises with the water or sewer line or both, and may fix charges for the connections. In lieu of requiring connection under this subsection and in order to avoid hardship, the city may require payment of a periodic availability charge, not to exceed the minimum periodic service charge for properties that are connected.

(b) Solid Waste. – A city may require an owner of improved property to do any of the following:

(1) Place solid waste in specified places or receptacles for the convenience of city collection and disposal.

(2) Separate materials before the solid waste is collected.

(3) Participate in a recycling program by requiring separation of designated materials by the owner or occupant of the property prior to disposal. An owner of recovered materials as defined by G.S. 130A-290(a)(24) retains ownership of the recovered materials until the owner conveys, sells, donates, or otherwise transfers the recovered materials to a person, firm, company, corporation, or unit of local government. A city may not require an owner to convey, sell, donate, or otherwise transfer recovered materials to the city or its designee. If an owner places recovered materials in receptacles or delivers recovered materials to specific locations, receptacles,

and facilities that are owned or operated by the city or its designee, then ownership of these materials is transferred to the city or its designee.

(4) Participate in any solid waste collection service provided by the city or by a person who has a contract with the city if the owner or occupant of the property has not otherwise contracted for the collection of solid waste from the property.

(c) A city may impose a fee for the solid waste collection service provided under subdivision (4) of subsection (b) of this section. The fee may not exceed the costs of collection. (1917, c. 136, subch. 7, s. 2; C.S., s. 2806; 1971, c. 698, s. 1; 1979, c. 619, s. 14: 1981, c. 823; 1989, c. 741, s. 2; 1991, c. 698, s. 2; 1993, c. 165, s. 2; 1995, c. 511, s. 4.)

§ 160A-318. Mutual aid contracts.

(a) Any two or more cities, counties, water and sewer authorities, metropolitan sewage districts, sanitary districts, or private utility companies or combination thereof may enter into contracts with each other to provide mutual aid and assistance in restoring electric, water, sewer, or gas services in the event of natural disasters or other emergencies under such terms and conditions as may be agreed upon. Mutual aid contracts may include provisions for furnishing personnel, equipment, apparatus, supplies and materials; for reimbursement or indemnification of the aiding party for loss or damage incurred by giving aid; for delegating authority to a designated official or employee to send aid upon request; and any other provisions not inconsistent with law.

(b) Officials and employees furnished by one party in aid of another party pursuant to a mutual aid contract entered into under authority of this section shall be conclusively deemed for all purposes to remain officials and employees of the aiding party. While providing aid to another and while traveling to and from another city or county pursuant to giving aid, they shall retain all rights, privileges, and immunities, including coverage under the North Carolina Workers' Compensation Act, as they enjoy while performing their normal duties.

(c) Notwithstanding any other provisions of law to the contrary, any party to a mutual aid contract entered into under authority of this section, may sell or otherwise convey or deliver to another party to the contract personal property to be used in restoring utility services pursuant to the contract, without following procedures for the sale or disposition of property prescribed by any general law, local act, or city charter.

(d)   Nothing in this section shall be construed to deprive any party to a mutual aid contract of its discretion to send or decline to send its personnel, equipment, and apparatus in aid of another party to the contract under any circumstances, whether or not obligated by the contract to do so. In no case shall a party to a mutual aid contract or any of its officials or employees be held to answer in any civil or criminal action for declining to send personnel, equipment, or apparatus to another party to the contract, whether or not obligated by contract to do so. (1967, c. 450; 1971, c. 698, s. 1; 1991, c. 636, s. 3.)

§ 160A-319. Utility franchises.

(a)   A city shall have authority to grant upon reasonable terms franchises for a telephone system and any of the enterprises listed in G.S. 160A-311, except a cable television system. A franchise granted by a city authorizes the operation of the franchised activity within the city. No franchise shall be granted for a period of more than 60 years, except that a franchise for solid waste collection or disposal systems and facilities shall not be granted for a period of more than 30 years. Except as otherwise provided by law, when a city operates an enterprise, or upon granting a franchise, a city may by ordinance make it unlawful to operate an enterprise without a franchise.

(b)   For the purposes of this section, "cable television system" means any system or facility that, by means of a master antenna and wires or cables, or by wires or cables alone, receives, amplifies, modifies, transmits, or distributes any television, radio, or electronic signal, audio or video or both, to subscribing members of the public for compensation. "Cable television system" does not include providing master antenna services only to property owned or leased by the same person, firm, or corporation, nor communication services rendered to a cable television system by a public utility that is regulated by the North Carolina Utilities Commission or the Federal Communications Commission in providing those services. (Code, ss. 704, 3117; 1901, c. 283; 1905, c. 526; Rev., s. 2916; 1907, c. 978; P.L. 1917, c. 223; C.S., s. 2623; Ex. Sess. 1921, c. 58; 1927, c. 14; 1933, c. 69; 1949, c. 938; 1955, c. 77; 1959, c. 391; 1961, c. 308; 1967, c. 100, s. 2; c. 1122, s. 1; 1969, c. 944; 1971, c. 698, s. 1; 1975, c. 664, s. 11; 1991 (Reg. Sess., 1992), c. 1013, s. 2; 2006-151, s. 15.)

§ 160A-320. Public enterprise improvements.

(a)   Authorization. – A city may contract with a developer or property owner, or with a private party who is under contract with the developer or property owner, for public enterprise improvements that are adjacent or ancillary to a private land development project. Such a contract shall allow the city to reimburse the private party for costs associated with the design and construction of improvements that are in addition to those required by the city's land development regulations. Such a contract is not subject to Article 8 of Chapter 143 of the General Statutes if the public cost will not exceed two hundred fifty thousand dollars ($250,000) and the city determines that: (i) the public cost will not exceed the estimated cost of providing for those improvements through either eligible force account qualified labor or through a public contract let pursuant to Article 8 of Chapter 143 of the General Statutes; or (ii) the coordination of separately constructed improvements would be impracticable. A city may enact ordinances and policies setting forth the procedures, requirements, and terms for agreements authorized by this section.

(b)   Property Acquisition. – The improvements may be constructed on property owned or acquired by the private party or on property owned or acquired by the city. The private party may assist the city in obtaining easements in favor of the city from private property owners on those properties that will be involved in or affected by the project. The contract between the city and the private party may be entered into before the acquisition of any real property necessary to the project. (2005-426, s. 8(d).)

§ 160A-321. Sale, lease, or discontinuance of city-owned enterprise.

A city is authorized to sell or lease as lessor any enterprise that it may own upon any terms and conditions that the council may deem best. However, except as to transfers to another governmental entity pursuant to G.S. 160A-274, a city-owned enterprise shall not be sold, leased to another, or discontinued unless the proposal to sell, lease, or discontinue is first submitted to a vote of the people and approved by a majority of those who vote thereon. Voter approval shall not be required for the sale, lease, or discontinuance of airports, off-street parking systems and facilities, or solid waste collection and disposal systems. (Code, ss. 704, 3117; 1901, c. 283; 1905, c. 526; Rev., s. 2916; 1907, c. 978; P.L. 1917, c. 223; C.S., s. 2623; Ex. Sess. 1921, c. 58; 1927, c. 14; 1933, c. 69; 1949, c. 938; 1955, c. 77; 1959, c. 391; 1961, c. 308; 1967, c. 100, s. 2; c. 1122, s. 1; 1969, c. 944; 1971, c. 698, s. 1; 1973, c. 489, s. 2.)

§ 160A-322. Contracts for electric power and water.

A city is authorized to enter into contracts for a period not exceeding 40 years for the supply of water, and for a period not exceeding 30 years for the supply of electric power or other public commodity or services. (Code, ss. 704, 3117; 1901, c. 283; 1905, c. 526; Rev., s. 2916; 1907, c. 978; P.L. 1917, c. 223; C.S., s. 2623; Ex. Sess. 1921, c. 58; 1927, c. 14; 1933, c. 69; 1949, c. 938; 1955, c. 77; 1959, c. 391; 1961, c. 308; 1967, c. 100, s. 2; c. 1122, s. 1; 1969, c. 944; 1971, c. 698, s. 1.)

§ 160A-323. Load management and peak load pricing of electric power.

In addition and supplemental to the powers conferred upon municipalities by the laws of the State and for the purposes of conserving electricity and increasing the economy of operation of municipal electric systems, any municipality owning or operating an electric distribution system, any municipality engaging in a joint project pursuant to Chapter 159B of the General Statutes and any joint agency created pursuant to Chapter 159B of the General Statutes, shall have and may exercise the power and authority:

(1)   To investigate, study, develop and place into effect procedures and to investigate, study, develop, purchase, lease, own, operate, maintain, and put into service devices, which will temporarily curtail or cut off certain types of appliances or equipment for short periods of time whenever an unusual peak demand threatens to overload the electric system or economies would result; and

(2)   To fix rates and bill customers by a system of nondiscriminatory peak pricing, with incentive rates for off-peak use of electricity charging more for peak periods than for off-peak periods to reflect the higher cost of providing electric service during periods of peak demand on the electric system. (1977, c. 232.)

§ 160A-324. Contract with private solid waste collection firm(s).

(a)   If the area to be annexed described in an act of the General Assembly includes an area where a firm (i) meets the requirements of subsection (a1) of this section, (ii) on the ninetieth day preceding the date of introduction in the House of Representatives or the Senate of the bill which became the act making the annexation, was providing solid waste collection services in the area to be annexed, (iii) is still providing such services on the date the act becomes law, and (iv) by reason of the annexation the firm's franchise with a county or arrangements with third parties for solid waste collection will be terminated, the city shall do one of the following:

> (1) Contract with the firm for a period of two years after the effective date of the annexation ordinance to allow the firm to provide collection services to the city in the area to be annexed for sums determined under subsection (d) of this section.

> (2) Pay the firm for the firm's economic loss, with one-third of the economic loss to be paid within 30 days of the termination and the balance paid in 12 equal monthly installments during the next succeeding 12 months. Any remaining economic loss payment is forfeited if the firm terminates service to customers in the annexation area prior to the effective date of the annexation.

> (3) Make other arrangements satisfactory to the parties.

(a1) To qualify for the options set forth in subsection (a) of this section, a firm must have, subsequent to receiving notice of the annexation in accordance with subsection (b) of this section, filed with the city clerk at least 10 days prior to the effective date of the annexation a written request to contract with the city to provide solid waste collection services containing a certification, signed by an officer or owner of the firm, that the firm serves at least 50 customers within the county at that time.

(a2) Firms shall file notice of provision of solid waste collection service with the city clerk of all cities located in the firm's collection area or within five miles thereof.

(b) The city shall make a good faith effort to provide at least 30 days before the effective date of the annexation a copy of the act to each private firm providing solid waste collection services in the area to be annexed. The notice shall be sent to all firms that filed notice in accordance with subsection (a2) of this section by certified mail, return receipt requested, to the address provided by the firm under subsection (a2) of this section.

(c) The city may require that the contract contain:

> (1) A requirement that the firm post a performance bond and maintain public liability insurance coverage;

(2)   A requirement that the firm agree to service customers in the annexed area that were not served by that firm on the effective date of annexation;

(3)   A provision that divides the annexed area into service areas if there were more than one firm being contracted within the area, such that the entire area is served by the firms, or by the city as to customers not served by the firms;

(4)   A provision that the city may serve customers not served by the firm on the effective date of annexation;

(5)   A provision that the contract can be cancelled in writing, delivered by certified mail to the firm in question with 30 days to cure, substantial violations of the contract, but no contract may be cancelled on these grounds unless the Local Government Commission finds that substantial violations have occurred, except that the city may suspend the contract for up to 30 days if it finds substantial violation of health laws;

(6)   Performance standards, not exceeding city standards existing at the time of notice provided pursuant to subsection (b) of this section, with provision that the contract may be cancelled for substantial violations of those standards, but no contract may be cancelled on those grounds unless the Local Government Commission finds that substantial violations have occurred;

(7)   A provision for monetary damages if there are violations of the contract or of performance standards.

(d)   If the services to be provided to the city by reason of the annexation are substantially the same as rendered under the franchise with the county or arrangements with the parties, the amount paid by the city shall be at least ninety percent (90%) of the amount paid or required under the existing franchise or arrangements. If such services are required to be adjusted to conform to city standards or as a result of changes in the number of customers and as a result there are changes in disposal costs (including mileage and landfill charges), requirements for storage capacity (dumpsters and/or residential carts), and/or frequency of collection, the amount paid by the city for the service shall be increased or decreased to reflect the value of such adjusted services as if computed under the existing franchise or arrangements. In the event agreement cannot be reached between the city and the firm under this subsection, the matters shall be determined by the Local Government Commission.

(e), (f) Repealed by Session Laws 2006-193, s. 1, applicable to annexations for which the bill making the annexation is enacted on or after January 1, 2007.

(g) If the city fails to offer a contract to the firm within 30 days following the effective date of the annexation act, the firm may appeal within 60 days following the effective date of the annexation act to the Local Government Commission for an order directing the city to offer a contract. If the Local Government Commission finds that the city has not made an offer which complies with this section, it shall order the city to pay to the firm a civil penalty of the amount of payments it finds that the city would have had to make under the contract, during the noncompliance period until the contract offer is made. Either the firm or the city may obtain judicial review in accordance with Chapter 150B of the General Statutes.

(h) A firm which has given notice under subsection (a) of this section that it desires to contract, and any firm that the city believes is eligible to give such notice, shall make available to the city not later than 30 days following a written request of the city all information in its possession or control, including but not limited to operational, financial and budgetary information, necessary for the city to determine if the firm qualifies for the benefits of this section and to determine the nature and scope of the potential contract and/or economic loss. The firm forfeits its rights under this section if it fails to make a good faith response within 30 days following receipt of the written request for information from the city, provided that the city's written request so states by specific reference to this section.

(i) As used in this section, the following terms mean:

    (1) Economic loss. – A sum equal to 15 times the average gross monthly revenue for the three months prior to the introduction of the bill under subsection (a) of this section, collected or due the firm for residential, commercial, and industrial collection service in the area annexed or to be annexed; provided that revenues shall be included in calculations under this subdivision only if policies of the city will provide solid waste collection to those customers such that arrangements between the firm and the customers will be terminated.

    (2) Firm. – A private solid waste collection firm. (1989, c. 598, s. 1; 2006-193, s. 3.)

§ 160A-325. Selection or approval of sites for certain sanitary landfills; solid waste defined.

(a)   The governing board of a city shall consider alternative sites and socioeconomic and demographic data and shall hold a public hearing prior to selecting or approving a site for a new sanitary landfill that receives residential solid waste that is located within one mile of an existing sanitary landfill within the State. The distance between an existing and a proposed site shall be determined by measurement between the closest points on the outer boundary of each site. The definitions set out in G.S. 130A-290 apply to this subsection. As used in this subsection:

    (1)   "Approving a site" refers to prior approval of a site under G.S. 130A-294(a)(4).

    (2)   "Existing sanitary landfill" means a sanitary landfill that is in operation or that has been in operation within the five-year period immediately prior to the date on which an application for a permit is submitted.

    (3)   "New sanitary landfill" means a sanitary landfill that includes areas not within the legal description of an existing sanitary landfill as set out in the permit for the existing sanitary landfill.

    (4)   "Socioeconomic and demographic data" means the most recent socioeconomic and demographic data compiled by the United States Bureau of the Census and any additional socioeconomic and demographic data submitted at the public hearing.

(b)   As used in this Part, "solid waste" means nonhazardous solid waste, that is, solid waste as defined in G.S. 130A-290 but not including hazardous waste. (1991 (Reg. Sess., 1992), c. 1013, s. 3.)

§ 160A-326. Limitations on rail transportation liability.

(a)   As used in this section:

    (1)   "Claim" means a claim, action, suit, or request for damages, whether compensatory, punitive, or otherwise, made by any person or entity against:

        a.   The City, a railroad, or an operating rights railroad; or

        b.   An officer, director, trustee, employee, parent, subsidiary, or affiliated corporation as defined in

G.S. 105-130.6, or agent of: the City, a railroad, or an operating rights railroad.

(2)   "Operating rights railroad" means a railroad corporation or railroad company that, prior to January 1, 2001, was granted operating rights by a State-Owned Railroad Company or operated over the property of a State-Owned Railroad Company under a claim of right over or adjacent to facilities used by or on behalf of the City.

(3)   "Passenger rail services" means the transportation of rail passengers by or on behalf of the City and all services performed by a railroad pursuant to a contract with the City in connection with the transportation of rail passengers, including, but not limited to, the operation of trains; the use of right-of-way, trackage, public or private roadway and rail crossings, equipment, or station areas or appurtenant facilities; the design, construction, reconstruction, operation, or maintenance of rail-related equipment, tracks, and any appurtenant facilities; or the provision of access rights over or adjacent to lines owned by the City or a railroad, or otherwise occupied by the City or a railroad, pursuant to charter grant, fee-simple deed, lease, easement, license, trackage rights, or other form of ownership or authorized use.

(4)   "Railroad" means a railroad corporation or railroad company, including a State-Owned Railroad Company as defined in G.S. 124-11, that has entered into any contracts or operating agreements of any kind with the City concerning passenger rail services.

(b)   Contracts Allocating Financial Responsibility Authorized. – The City may contract with any railroad to allocate financial responsibility for passenger rail services claims, including, but not limited to, the execution of indemnity agreements, notwithstanding any other statutory, common law, public policy, or other prohibition against same, and regardless of the nature of the claim or the conduct giving rise to such claim.

(c)   Insurance Required. –

(1)   If the City enters into any contract authorized by subsection (b) of this section, the contract shall require the City to secure and maintain, upon and after the commencement

of the operation of trains by or on behalf of the City, a liability insurance policy covering the liability of the parties to the contract, a State-Owned Railroad Company as defined in G.S. 124-11 that owns or claims an interest in any real property subject to the contract, and any operating rights railroad for all claims for property damage, personal injury, bodily injury, and death arising out of or related to passenger rail services. The policy shall name the parties to the contract, a State-Owned Railroad Company as defined in G.S. 124-11 that owns or claims an interest in any real property subject to the contract, and any operating rights railroad as named insureds and shall have policy limits of not less than two hundred million dollars ($200,000,000) per single accident or incident, and may include a self-insured retention in an amount of not more than five million dollars ($5,000,000).

(2)   If the City does not enter into any contract authorized by subsection (b) of this section, upon and after the commencement of the operation of trains by or on behalf of the City, the City shall secure and maintain a liability insurance policy, with policy limits and a self-insured retention consistent with subdivision (1) of this subsection, for all claims for property damage, personal injury, bodily injury, and death arising out of or related to passenger rail services.

(d)   Liability Limit. – The aggregate liability of the City, the parties to the contract or contracts authorized by subsection (b) of this section, a State-Owned Railroad Company as defined in G.S. 124-11, and any operating rights railroad for all claims arising from a single accident or incident related to passenger rail services for property damage, personal injury, bodily injury, and death is limited to two hundred million dollars ($200,000,000) per single accident or incident or to any proceeds available under any insurance policy secured pursuant to subsection (c) of this section, whichever is greater.

(e)   Effect on Other Laws. – This section shall not affect the damages that may be recovered under the Federal Employers' Liability Act, 45 U.S.C. § 51, et seq., (1908); or under Article 1 of Chapter 97 of the General Statutes.

(f)   Applicability. – This section shall apply only to municipalities with a population of more than 500,000 persons, according to the latest decennial census, or to municipalities that have entered into a transit governance interlocal agreement with, among other local governments, a city with a population of more than 500,000 persons. (2002-78, s. 3.)

§ 160A-327. Displacement of private solid waste collection services.

(a)   A unit of local government shall not displace a private company that is providing collection services for municipal solid waste or recovered materials, or both, except as provided for in this section.

(b)   Before a local government may displace a private company that is providing collection services for municipal solid waste or recovered materials, or both, the unit of local government shall publish notice of the first meeting where the proposed change in solid waste collection service will be discussed. Notice shall be published once a week for at least four consecutive weeks in at least one newspaper of general circulation in the area in which the unit of local government and the proposed displacement area are located. The first public notice shall be given no less than 30 days but no more than 60 days prior to the displacement issue being placed on the agenda for discussion or action at an official meeting of the governing body of the unit of local government. The notice shall specify the date and place of the meeting, the geographic location in which solid waste collection services are proposed to be changed, and the types of solid waste collection services that may be affected. In addition, the unit of local government shall send written notice by certified mail, return receipt requested, to all companies that have filed notice with the unit of local government clerk pursuant to the provisions of subsection (f) of this section. The unit of local government shall deposit notice in the U.S. mail at least 30 days prior to the displacement issues being placed on the agenda for discussion or action at an official meeting of the governing body of the unit of local government.

(c)   Following the public notice required by subsection (b) of this section, but in no event later than six months after the date of the first meeting pursuant to subsection (b) of this section, the unit of local government may proceed to take formal action to displace a private company. The unit of local government or other public or private entity selected by the unit of local government may not commence the actual provision of these services for a period of 15 months from the date of the first publication of notice, unless the unit of local government provides compensation to the displaced private company as follows:

(1)   Subject to subdivision (3) of this subsection, if the private company has provided collection services in the displacement area prior to announcement of the displacement action, the unit of local government shall provide compensation to the displaced private company in an amount equal to the total gross revenues for collection services provided in the displacement area for the six months prior to the first publication of notice required under subsection (b) of this section.

(2)   Subject to subdivision (3) of this subsection, if the displaced private company has provided collection services in the displacement area for less than six months prior to the first publication of notice required under subsection (b) of this section, the unit of local government shall provide compensation to the displaced private company in an amount equal to the total gross revenues for the period of time that the private company provided such services in the displacement area.

(3)   If the displaced private company purchased an existing operation of another private company providing such services, compensation shall be for six months based on the monthly average total gross revenues for three months the immediate preceding the first publication of notice required under subsection (b) of this section.

(d)   If the local government elects to provide compensation pursuant to subsection (c) of this section, the amount due from the unit of local government to the displaced company shall be paid as follows: one-third of the compensation to be paid within 30 days of the displacement and the balance paid in six equal monthly installments during the next succeeding six months.

(e)   If the unit of local government fails to change the provision of solid waste services as described in the notices required under subsection (b) of this section within six months of the date of the first meeting pursuant to subsection (b) of this section, the unit of local government shall not take action to displace without complying again with the provisions of subsection (b) of this section.

(f)   Notice of the provision of solid waste collection service shall be filed with the unit of local government clerk of all cities and counties located in the private company's collection area or within five miles thereof.

(g)　This section shall not apply when a private company is displaced as the result of an annexation under Article 4A of Chapter 160A of the General Statutes or an annexation by an act of the General Assembly. The provisions of G.S. 160A-37.3, 160-49.3, or 160A-324 shall apply.

(h)　If a unit of local government intends to provide compensation under subsection (c) of this section to a private company that has given notice under subsection (f) of this section, the private company shall make available to the unit of local government not later than 30 days following a written request of the unit of local government, sent by certified mail, return receipt requested, all information in its possession or control, including operational, financial, and budgetary information necessary for the unit of local government to determine if the private company qualifies for compensation. The private company forfeits its rights under this section if it fails to make a good faith response within 30 days following receipt of the written request for information from the unit of local government provided that the unit of local government's written request so states by specific reference to this section.

(i)　Nothing in this section shall affect the authority of a city or county to establish recycling service where recycling service is not currently being offered.

(j)　As used in this section, the following terms mean:

(1)　Collection. – The gathering of municipal solid waste, recovered materials, or recyclables from residential, commercial, industrial, governmental, or institutional customers and transporting it to a sanitary landfill or other disposal facility. Collection does not include transport from a transfer station or processing point to a disposal facility.

(2)　Displacement. – Any formal action by a unit of local government that prohibits a private company from providing all or a portion of the collection services for municipal solid waste, recovered materials, or recyclables that the company is providing in the affected area at least 90 days prior to the date of the first publication of notice required by subsection (b) of this section. Displacement also means an action by a unit of local government to use an availability fee, nonoptional fee, or taxes to fund competing collection services for municipal solid waste, recovered materials, or recyclables that the private company is providing in the affected areas at least 90 days prior to the date of the first publication of notice required under subsection (b) of this section is given. Displacement does not include any of the following actions:

a. Failure to renew a franchise agreement or contract with a private company.

b. Taking action that results in a change in solid waste collection services because the private company's operations present an imminent and substantial threat to human health or safety or are causing a substantial public nuisance.

c. Taking action that results in a change in solid waste collection services because the private company has materially breached its franchise agreement or the terms of a contract with the local government, or the company has notified the local government that it no longer intends to honor the terms of the franchise agreement or contract. Notice of breach must be delivered in writing, delivered by certified mail to the firm in question with 30 days to cure the violation of the contract.

d. Terminating an existing contract or franchise in accordance with the provisions of the contract or franchise agreement.

e. Providing temporary collection services under a declared state of emergency.

f. Taking action that results in a change in solid waste collection services due to the existing providers' felony conviction of a violation in the State of federal or State law governing the solid waste collection or disposal.

g. Contracting with a private company to continue its existing services or provide a different level of service at a negotiated price on terms agreeable to the parties.

(3) Municipal solid waste. – As defined in G.S. 130A-290(18a).

(4) Unit of local government. – A county, municipality, authority, or political subdivision that is authorized by law to provide for collection of solid waste or recovered materials, or both. (2006-193, s. 4.)

§ 160A-328. Local government landfill liaison.

(a)   A city that has planning jurisdiction over any portion of the site of a sanitary landfill may employ a local government landfill liaison. No person who is responsible for any aspect of the management or operation of the landfill may serve as a local government landfill liaison. A local government landfill liaison shall have a right to enter public or private lands on which the landfill facility is located at reasonable times to inspect the landfill operation in order to:

  (1)   Ensure that the facility meets all local requirements.
  (2)   Identify and notify the Department of suspected violations of applicable federal or State laws, regulations, or rules.
  (3)   Identify and notify the Department of potentially hazardous conditions at the facility.

(b)   Entry pursuant to this section shall not constitute a trespass or taking of property. (2007-550, s. 11(b).)

§ 160A-329. Reserved for future codification purposes.

§ 160A-330. Reserved for future codification purposes.

Part 2. Electric Service in Urban Areas.

§ 160A-331. Definitions.

Unless the context otherwise requires, the following words and phrases shall have the meanings indicated when used in this Part:

  (1)   "Assigned area" means any portion of an area annexed to or incorporated into a city which, on or before the effective date of annexation or incorporation, had been assigned by the North Carolina Utilities Commission to a specific electric supplier pursuant to G.S. 62-110.2.

  (1a)   "Assigned supplier" means a person, firm, or corporation to which the North Carolina Utilities Commission had assigned a specific area for service as an electric supplier pursuant to G.S. 62-110.2, which area, in whole or in part, is subsequently annexed to or incorporated into a city.

  (1b)   The "determination date" is

    a.   April 20, 1965, with respect to areas within the corporate limits of any city as of April 20, 1965;

b.   The effective date of annexation with respect to areas annexed to any city after April 20, 1965;

c.   The date a primary supplier comes into being with respect to any city first incorporated after April 20, 1965.

(2)   "Line" means any conductor located inside the city, or any conductor within 300 feet of areas annexed by the city that is a primary supplier, for distributing or transmitting electricity, except as follows:

a.   For overhead construction, a conductor from the pole nearest the premises of a consumer to such premises, or a conductor from a line tap to such premises.

b.   For underground construction, a conductor from the transformer (or the junction point, if there be one) nearest the premises of a consumer to such premises.

(3)   "Premises" means the building, structure, or facility to which electricity is being or is to be furnished. Two or more buildings, structures, or facilities that are located on one tract or contiguous tracts of land and are used by one electric consumer for commercial, industrial, institutional, or governmental purposes, shall together constitute one "premises," except that any such building, structure, or facility shall not, together with any other building, structure, or facility, constitute one "premises" if the electric service to it is separately metered and the charges for such service are calculated independently of charges for service to any other building, structure, or facility.

(4)   "Primary supplier" means a city that owns and maintains its own electric system, or a person, firm, or corporation that furnishes electric service within a city pursuant to a franchise granted by, or contract with, a city, or that, having furnished service pursuant to a franchise or contract, is continuing to furnish service within a city after the expiration of the franchise or contract.

(5)   "Secondary supplier" means a person, firm, or corporation that is not a primary supplier, but that furnishes electricity at

retail to one or more consumers other than itself within the limits of a city, or that has a conductor located within 300 feet of an area annexed by a city that is a primary supplier. A primary supplier that furnishes electric service within a city pursuant to a franchise or contract that limits or restricts the classes of consumers or types of electric service permitted to such supplier shall, in and with respect to any area annexed by the city after April 20, 1965, be a primary supplier for such classes of consumers or types of service, and if it furnishes other electric service in the annexed area on the effective date of annexation, shall be a secondary supplier, in and with respect to such annexed area, for all other electric service. A primary supplier that continues to furnish electric service after the expiration of a franchise or contract that limited or restricted such primary supplier with respect to classes of consumers or types of electric service shall, in and with respect to any area annexed by the city after April 20, 1965, be a secondary supplier for all electric service if it is furnishing electric service in the annexed area on the effective date of annexation. (1965, c. 287, s. 1; 1971, c. 698, s. 1; 1973, c. 426, s. 52; 1997-346, s. 1; 1999-111, s. 1; 2003-24, s. 1; 2005-150, s. 2.)

§ 160A-331.1: Repealed by Session Laws 2007-419, s. 3, effective August 21, 2007.

§ 160A-331.2. Agreements of electric suppliers.

(a)   The General Assembly finds and determines that, in order to avoid the unnecessary duplication of electric facilities and to facilitate the settlement of disputes between cities that are primary suppliers and other electric suppliers, it is desirable for the State to authorize electric suppliers to enter into agreements pursuant to which the parties to the agreements allocate to each other the right to provide electric service to premises each would not have the right to serve under this Article but for the agreement, provided that no agreement between a city that is a primary supplier and another electric supplier shall be enforceable by or against an electric supplier that is subject to the territorial assignment jurisdiction of the North Carolina Utilities Commission until the agreement has been approved by the Commission. The

Commission shall approve an agreement entered into pursuant to this section unless it finds that such agreement is not in the public interest. Such agreements may allocate the right to serve premises by reference to specific premises, geographical boundaries, or amounts of unspecified load to be served, but no agreement shall affect in any way the rights of other electric suppliers who are not parties to the relevant agreement. The provisions of this section apply to agreements relating to electric service inside and outside the corporate limits of a city.

(b)   Repealed by Session Laws 2007-419, s. 1, effective August 21, 2007.

(c)   To the extent negotiations undertaken pursuant to subsection (b) of this section, as enacted by S.L. 2005-150, have not resulted in an agreement between a negotiating electric membership corporation and a negotiating city by May 31, 2007, jurisdiction shall immediately lie in the North Carolina Utilities Commission to resolve all issues related to those negotiations. Either party to the negotiations may petition the Commission to exercise the jurisdiction conferred in this subsection upon the filing of a petition and the payment of a filing fee of five hundred dollars ($500.00). In reaching its decision, the Commission shall include consideration of the public convenience and necessity. The Commission shall not consider rate differentials between the involved city and the involved electric membership corporation.

(d)   Notwithstanding an order of the Commission issued pursuant to subsection (c) of this section:

   (1)   Any electric membership corporation or city may furnish electric service to any consumer who desires service from that electric membership corporation or city at any premises being served by another electric membership corporation or city, or at premises which another electric membership corporation or city has the right to serve pursuant to subsection (c) of this section, upon agreement of the affected electric membership corporation or city, subject to approval by the Commission.

   (2)   The Commission shall have the authority and jurisdiction, after notice to all affected electric membership corporations and cities and after a hearing, if a hearing is requested by any affected electric membership corporation or city, or any other interested party, to order any electric membership corporation or city which may reasonably do so to furnish electric service to any consumer who desires service from

that electric membership corporation or city at any premises being served by another electric membership corporation or city pursuant to subsection (c) of this section or subdivision (1) of this subsection, or which another electric membership corporation or city has the right to serve pursuant to subsection (c) of this section or subdivision (1) of this subsection, and to order the other electric membership corporation or city to cease and desist from furnishing electric service to such premises, upon finding that service to the consumer by the electric membership corporation or city which is then furnishing service, or which has the right to furnish service to those premises, is or will be inadequate or undependable, or that the rates, conditions of service, or service regulations, applied to such consumer, are unreasonably discriminatory.

(e)   Assignments or reassignments made or approved by the Commission pursuant to subsection (c) or (d) of this section shall be deemed to be service area agreements approved pursuant to subsection (a) of this section. (2005-150, s. 3; 2007-419, s. 1.)

§ 160A-332. Electric service within city limits.

(a)   The suppliers of electric service inside the corporate limits of any city in which a secondary supplier was furnishing electric service on the determination date (as defined in G.S. 160A-331(1)) shall have rights and be subject to restrictions as follows:

(1)   The secondary supplier shall have the right to serve all premises being served by it, or to which any of its facilities are attached, on the determination date.

(2)   The secondary supplier shall have the right, subject to subdivision (3) of this section, to serve all premises initially requiring electric service after the determination date which are located wholly within 300 feet of its lines and located wholly more than 300 feet from the lines of the primary supplier, as such suppliers' lines existed on the determination date.

(3)   Any premises initially requiring electric service after the determination date which are located wholly within 300 feet of a secondary supplier's lines and wholly within 300 feet

of another secondary supplier's lines, but wholly more than 300 feet from the primary supplier's lines, as the lines of all suppliers existed on the determination date, may be served by the secondary supplier which the consumer chooses, and no other supplier shall thereafter furnish electric service to such premises, except with the written consent of the supplier then serving the premises.

(4)   A primary supplier shall not furnish electric service to any premises which a secondary supplier has the right to serve as set forth in subdivisions (1), (2), and (3) of this section, except with the written consent of the secondary supplier.

(5)   Any premises initially requiring electric service after the determination date which are located wholly or partially within 300 feet of the primary supplier's lines and are located wholly or partially within 300 feet of the secondary supplier's lines, as such suppliers' lines existed on the determination date, may be served by either the secondary supplier or the primary supplier, whichever the consumer chooses, and no other supplier shall thereafter furnish service to such premises, except with the written consent of the supplier then serving the premises.

(6)   Any premises initially requiring electric service after the determination date, which are located only partially within 300 feet of the secondary supplier's lines and are located wholly more than 300 feet from the primary supplier's lines, as such supplier's lines existed on the determination date, may be served either by the secondary supplier or the primary supplier, whichever the consumer chooses, and no other supplier shall thereafter furnish service to such premises, except with the written consent of the supplier then serving the premises.

(6a)   Notwithstanding any other provision of law, a secondary supplier, upon obtaining the prior written consent of the city, shall be the exclusive provider of electric service within (i) any assigned area for which that secondary supplier had been assigned supplier prior to the determination date; or (ii) any area previously unassigned by the North Carolina Utilities Commission pursuant to G.S. 62-110.2. However, any rights of other electric suppliers existing under G.S. 62-110.2 prior to the determination date to provide service shall continue to exist without impairment in the areas described in (i) and (ii) above.

(6b) A primary supplier or secondary supplier that, after the determination date, offers to serve any premises initially requiring electric service for which a consumer has a right to choose suppliers under subsections (5) or (6) of this section, without providing the consumer written notice that the consumer may be entitled to choose another electric supplier for the premises, shall not have the right to serve those premises.

(7) Except as provided in subdivisions (1), (2), (3), (5), (6), and (6a) of this section, a secondary supplier shall not furnish electric service within the corporate limits of any city unless it first obtains the written consent of the city and the primary supplier.

(b) In any city that is first incorporated after April 20, 1965, in which, on the effective date of the incorporation, there is more than one supplier of electric service, all suppliers of electric service therein shall continue to have the rights and be subject to the restrictions in effect before the city was incorporated until there is a primary supplier within the city.

(c) It shall be unlawful for a primary supplier or secondary supplier to serve premises within a city that the supplier does not have the right to serve under the provisions of this Article. Upon receiving written notice from another supplier of electric service that has authority to lawfully provide service to the premises in dispute that the provision of service by the current supplier is unlawful, the primary supplier or secondary supplier that is providing electric service shall be obligated to discontinue service and remove all of its facilities used in the provision of the unlawful service within 30 days after substitute electric service can be provided by an electric supplier with authority to lawfully provide service to the premises, unless the supplier currently providing service has a good faith basis for believing it has authority to continue rendering such service. If the primary or secondary supplier is determined to be providing electric services unlawfully, and is found to have unreasonably failed to fulfill its obligation to discontinue service as required above, the supplier of electric service that has authority to lawfully provide service to the premises may bring an action to compel performance of those obligations, and may recover in that action its costs of enforcing this subsection, including its reasonable attorneys' fees. (1965, c. 287, s. 1; 1971, c. 698, s. 1; 1997-346, s. 2; 1999-111, s. 1; 2003-24, s. 1; 2005-150, ss. 4, 5.)

§ 160A-333. Temporary electric service.

No electric supplier shall furnish temporary electric service for the construction of premises which it would not have the right to serve under this Part if such premises were already constructed. The construction of lines for, and the furnishing of, temporary electric service for the construction of premises which any other electric supplier, if chosen by the consumer, would have the right to serve if such premises were already constructed, shall not impair the right of such other electric supplier to furnish service to such premises after the construction thereof, if then chosen by the consumer; nor, unless the consumer chooses to have such premises served by the supplier that furnished the temporary service, shall the furnishing of such temporary service or the construction of a line therefor impair the right of any other electric supplier to furnish service to any other premises which, without regard to the construction of such temporary service line, it has the right to serve. (1965, c. 287, s. 1; 1971, c. 698, s. 1; 1973, c. 426, s. 53.)

§ 160A-334. Authority and jurisdiction of Utilities Commission.

Notwithstanding G.S. 160A-332 and 160A-333, if the North Carolina Utilities Commission finds that service being furnished to or to be furnished to the consumer by a secondary supplier is or will be inadequate or undependable, or that rates, conditions of service or service regulations, applied to such consumer, are unreasonably discriminatory, the Commission shall have the authority and jurisdiction, after notice to each affected electric supplier, and after hearing, if a hearing is requested by an interested party, to:

    (1)   Order a primary supplier that is subject to the jurisdiction of the Commission to furnish electric service to any consumer who desires service from the primary supplier at any premises served by a secondary supplier, or at premises which a secondary supplier has the right to serve pursuant to other sections of this Part, and to order such secondary supplier to cease and desist from furnishing electric service to such premises, or

    (2)   Order any secondary supplier to cease and desist from furnishing electric service to any premises being served by it or to any premises which it has the right to serve pursuant to

other sections of this Part, if the consumer desires service from a primary supplier that is not subject to the jurisdiction of the Commission and which is willing to furnish service to such premises. (1965, c. 287, s. 1; 1971, c. 698, s. 1; 1973, c. 426, s. 54.)

§ 160A-335. Discontinuance of service and transfer of facilities by secondary supplier.

A secondary supplier may voluntarily discontinue its service to any premises and remove any of its electric facilities located inside the corporate limits of a city or sell and transfer such facilities to a primary supplier in such city, subject to approval by the North Carolina Utilities Commission, if the Commission determines that the public interest will not thereby be adversely affected. (1965, c. 287, s. 1; 1971, c. 698, s. 1.)

§ 160A-336. Electric service for city facilities.

No provisions of this Part shall prevent a city that is a primary supplier from furnishing its own electric service for city facilities, or prevent any other primary supplier from furnishing electric street lighting service to a city inside its corporate limits. (1965, c. 287, s. 1; 1971, c. 698, s. 1.)

§ 160A-337. Effect of Part on rights and duties of primary supplier.

Except for the rights granted to and restrictions upon primary suppliers contained in the provisions of this Part, nothing in this Part shall diminish, enlarge, alter, or affect in any way the rights and duties of a primary supplier to furnish electric service to premises within the corporate limits of a city. (1965, c. 287, s. 1; 1971, c. 698, s. 1.)

§ 160A-338. Electric suppliers subject to police power.

No provisions of this Part shall restrict the exercise of the police power of a city over the erection and maintenance of poles, wires, and other facilities of electric suppliers in streets, alleys, and other public ways. (1965, c. 287, s. 1; 1971, c. 698, s. 1.)

§§ 160A-339 through 160A-340. Reserved for future codification purposes.

Index

B

bankruptcy filings

    deposit or security fee applied to delinquent payment, 85

    discontinuation of services and

        authority to discontinue services, 51

        delinquencies after filing, 68–69

        delinquencies prior to filing, 65–67

        types of, 65n45

billing practices, 23–30

    administrative fees, 29–30

    another local government contracted for services, 27–28

    mailing and delivery, 27–28

    multiple fees on one bill, 23–24, 63–64, 78

    non-utility taxes and fees included on utility bill, 24

    overbilling, 49, 90

    payment methods, 28–30

    postcard form, use of, 26

    private entities contracting to provide services, 27

    property taxes, billing utilities with. *See* property taxes, billing solid waste services with

    returned checks and rejected debit payments, fees on, 82–83

    Social Security number, use of, 25, 26

    specific information provided on bills, 28

    timely bill, failure to provide, 47–48

    transaction or processing fees, 29

    underbilled amounts, 43–46

building code, refusal to reconnect or establish account at properties not meeting, 12

C

code, refusal to reconnect or establish account at properties not meeting, 12

collection agencies, 79, 83

collection methods. *See* billing practices; delinquent payment

confidentiality. *See* privacy and confidentiality

connection to water/wastewater services

    availability fees, 14–17, 32, 34–38, 84

requiring, 14–15

tap fee deposit, 84

constitution, North Carolina. *See* North Carolina constitution

Constitution, U.S.

due process clause, 53–54, 56n18, 58, 69

equal protection clause, 11, 14

property interest in utility services, 53–54, 55–57n18–19

contract for services

implied contract/quasi-contract theory, 39–43

services provided without

to individuals or nongovernment entities, 39–41

to local government entities, 41–42

to state or federal government entities, 42–43

tenant or occupant as third-party beneficiary to, 53

credit card payments, 28–30

credit checks, 21

criminal enforcement on delinquent payment, 81–82

D

damages

failure to provide services, liability for, 52, 55–57n18

illegal reconnection following discontinuation of services, 90

wrongful disconnection, liability for, 59, 69

debit card payments, 28–30

delinquent payment, 73–87

availability fees, 84

bankrupts. *See* bankruptcy filings

collection agencies, 79, 83

criminal enforcement, 81–82

debt setoff program, 73–76

deposit or security fees

applied to unpaid amount, 84–85

charged due to nonpayment, 8

discontinuation of services due to. *See* discontinuation of services

extinguishment of debt, 79–80

failure to pursue legal remedies for collection, 71

interest on, 85

S

sale of goods, provision of water services as, 40n9

sanitation, utility fees for. *See* utility fees

schools, remittance of late fees to, 81–82

second notices, 58–59

security fees. *See* deposit or security fees

segregation of monies held as deposit or security fees, 6

Setoff Debt Collection Act, 74n6

sewage services, utility fees for. *See* utility fees

Social Security numbers

    account, required to establish, 2–3

    bill, inclusion on, 25, 26

    debt setoff program and, 75, 76

    deposit or security fee required due to failure to provide, 5

    privacy and confidentiality of, 1–3, 25, 26

solid waste services, utility fees for. *See* utility fees

sovereign immunity, 41–43, 69

Standard Mail versus First Class, 27

state constitution. *See* North Carolina constitution

state government entities

    contract, collection for services provided without, 42–43

    sovereign immunity, 41–43, 69

State Privacy Act, 2, 5

statute of limitations

    delinquent payment, attempts to collect

        solid waste fees, 78–79

        waiver of statute on customer reaffirmation of debt owed, 77

        wastewater fees, 77–78

        water fees, 76–77

    implied contracts, 40–41

    overbilling, 49, 90

    timely bill, failure to provide, 47–48

    underbilled amounts, 45–46

www.ingramcontent.com/pod-product-compliance
Lightning Source LLC
Chambersburg PA
CBHW061321220326
41599CB00026B/4974